200 *Fast*
food for friends

200 *Fast*
food for friends

hamlyn **all color**

Standard level kitchen cup and spoon measurements
are used in all recipes.

Ovens should be preheated to the specified temperature;
if using a convection oven, follow the manufacturer's
instructions for adjusting the time and temperature.

Fresh herbs should be used unless otherwise stated.

Eggs should be large unless otherwise stated. The
U.S. Food And Drug Administration advises that eggs
should not be consumed raw. This book contains dishes
made with raw or lightly cooked eggs. It is prudent for more
vulnerable people, such as pregnant and nursing mothers,
people with weakened immune systems, the elderly, babies,
and young children, to avoid uncooked or lightly cooked
dishes made with eggs. Once prepared, these dishes
should be kept refrigerated and used promptly.

This book includes dishes made with nuts and
nut derivatives. It is advisable for customers with known
allergic reactions to nuts and nut derivatives and those who
may be potentially vulnerable to these allergies, such as
pregnant and nursing mothers, people with a weakened
immune system, the elderly, babies, and children, to avoid
dishes made with nuts and nut oils. It is also prudent to
check the labels of prepared ingredients for the possible
inclusion of nut derivatives.

4

contents

introduction

This book offers a new and flexible approach to planning meals for busy cooks and lets you choose the recipe option that best fits the time you have available. Here, you will find more than 200 dishes that will inspire and motivate you to get cooking every day of the year.

All the recipes take a maximum of 30 minutes to cook. Some take as little as 20 minutes and, amazingly, many take only 10 minutes.

On every page, you'll find a main recipe plus a short-cut version or a fancier variation if you have a little more time on hand. Whatever you go for, you'll find a huge range of superquick recipes to get you through the week.

food for friends

Inviting friends and family over for a bite to eat should be the easiest, most enjoyable thing in the world, but too often most of your time is spent slaving in the kitchen instead of having fun and enjoying dinner together. But it's easy to produce delicious, inspiring dishes in less than 30 minutes, and some are so simple they can be on the table in just 10 minutes. Which lets you get on with the important things in life.

get ahead

A little planning ahead is always useful when having friends over. Try to think of your guests'

tastes—find out if you need to cater for any special diets or if there is something people especially love to eat—and then decide on your main dish. Once you've worked this out, it's easier to decide what else to serve.

Think about timings when planning what you eat. For a larger meal, it's useful to actually write down a schedule of when things need to be started. However, no matter the scale of your event, it's always best to cook a few delicious dishes instead of being stressed and trying to organize an array of mediocre ones. It's a good idea to focus your effort on one dish, so if you choose a complicated appetizer, keep the main dish simple with something like pasta. If you opt for a show-off dessert and main dish, make the appetizer a no-cook salad. When planning your menu, make sure that you think about the washing up. You don't want to be cleaning up the kitchen for hours after your guests have left, so wash up as you go along. If time is really short, cook a one-dish meal; an attractive flameproof casserole dish that can be taken straight from the stove to the table is a great investment and makes for a relaxing meal.

in-law—and this book includes a tempting range of simple appetizer recipes. On other occasions, it is perfectly acceptable to abandon formal appetizers and set out a selection of nuts, olives, and good-quality potato chips, served with a cocktail or glass of bubbly. You could provide more substantial nibbles to which guests can help themselves, such as hams and salami, olives, marinated artichokes, and so on.

stress-free cooking

appetizers

A sit-down appetizer sets the scene for a formal evening—perhaps a birthday dinner or when you want to impress the parents-

main dishes

There are plenty of ways of keeping the main dish simple and quick. A leg or shoulder of lamb will take quite a while to cook in the oven, but a rack of lamb can be on the table

in less than 30 minutes. This makes life easy, but remember that with these leaner, quick-cooking cuts of meat, it really is worthwhile spending a little extra to get the best quality—you will taste the difference. Fish and seafood are perfect for the host in a hurry, because they take so little time to cook and need not much more than a squeeze of lemon juice and simple side dish to turn them into a delicious dinner-party treat. However, shop for them on the day you are planning to cook them, because fresh fish really does taste better.

Vegetarians can sometimes feel cheated at dinner parties, so to make a meal really special, look for seasonal ingredients—the first asparagus of the season or a perfectly ripe bunch of tomatoes are great starting points for a meat-free meal. More unusual heritage vegetables or baby vegetables are also a wonderful way of perking up a plate and making it look worthy of a restaurant.

The flavor of good-quality basic ingredients will always shine through, and all it takes to enhance them is a little fresh pesto, a drizzle of a special oil or vinegar, or a sprinkling of fresh herbs. Keep side dishes simple and fast; a selection of greens dressed with something special, or maybe some couscous, which can be ready in only 5 minutes. Make the most of canned beans, which can be easily blended to make quick mashed beans or you can toss them with some dressing and tomatoes to create a hearty salad.

Another way to make the meal a little more special is to use an unusual ingredient. Supermarkets are increasingly catering for more exotic tastes and an exciting ingredient can elevate a meal to something more memorable. Look out for jewel-like pomegranate seeds, which look pretty on the plate and are great to sprinkle over salads or Middle Eastern dishes. For an Asian dish, try some authentic ingredients, such as lime leaves and lemon grass, which will lend your dish a beautifully subtle and distinctive flavor, or track down a good-quality curry paste. If you're making a simple Italian supper, search out a different type of pasta than you usually use—perhaps try thick tubelike bucatini or use black squid-ink pasta for a seafood dish. Sometimes it is worth spending a little extra on a key ingredient that can be used sparingly. Creamy buffalo mozzarella is a world apart from the regular cow milk version, while just a hint of perfumed saffron will transform a paella. It's also worth remembering that a splash of alcohol can lift a dish—brandy or wine for a French dish, a drop of vermouth for fish, or sherry for a Spanish feel.

dessert
To round off the meal in style, you'll want to prepare something delectable, but that doesn't mean it has to be complicated. Browse through the dessert recipes for inspiration, choosing a 10-minute recipe if you are short on time. Or for a really stress-free evening, serve a selection of great cheeses with some walnuts, crackers, grapes, and perhaps a bottle of sweet wine, or a colorful bowl of exotic fruit salad.

what to do if it all goes wrong
Even the best, most experienced cook will have nights when things go wrong in the kitchen. The most important thing is not to panic. A relaxed, welcoming host is what makes the evening. And the chances are that no one will notice anyway—a name change is often all that is needed.

appetizers & light bites

bloody mary gazpacho

OPTIONAL

Serves **4**

Total cooking time **10 minutes**

2 **garlic cloves**, chopped

2 **celery sticks**, chopped, plus
  extra, preferably with leaves,
  to serve

1 tablespoon chopped **onion**

4 **ripe tomatoes** (about 1 lb)

1 ¼ cups **tomato juice**

juice of **2 limes**

1 teaspoon **celery salt**

2–3 tablespoons
  Worcestershire sauce

½ cup **vodka** (optional)

Tabasco sauce, to taste

To serve

lime wedges

ice cubes

Put all the ingredients, except the vodka and Tabasco sauce, into a food processor or blender and process until smooth. Press the mixture through a fine-mesh strainer to remove all the tomato pulp.

Add the vodka, if using, and Tabasco sauce to taste, then pour into glasses filled with some ice cubes. Serve with celery sticks and lime wedges for squeezing over the top.

For roasted tomato gazpacho, toss 4 halved tomatoes (about 1 lb) with 3 tablespoons olive oil. Put into a roasting pan with 2 peeled garlic cloves and cook in a preheated oven, at 400°F, for 20 minutes or until soft and lightly browned. Place in a food processor or blender with 1 drained roasted red pepper from a jar, 2 teaspoons sherry vinegar, 1 crustless slice of bread, and 1 ¼ cups tomato juice and process until smooth. Rub through a fine-mesh strainer to remove all the tomato pulp, then season and add a little Tabasco sauce to taste. Chill in the freezer for 5 minutes, then ladle into serving bowls. Sprinkle with 1 tablespoon chopped red onion mixed together with 1 pitted, peeled, and diced avocado. **Total cooking time 30 minutes.**

corn cakes with smoked salmon

Serves **4**

Total cooking time **20 minutes**

2 **eggs**, beaten

¼ cup **milk**

1 (11 oz) can **corn kernels**, drained

⅔ cup **all-purpose flour**

½ teaspoon **baking powder**

2 **scallions**, sliced

2 tablespoons **vegetable oil**

5 oz **smoked salmon**

¼ cup **mascarpone cheese**

salt and **black pepper**

chopped **chives**, to garnish

Beat together the eggs, milk, corn, flour, baking powder, and scallions in a bowl until you have a smooth batter. Season well.

Heat 1 tablespoon of the oil in a large, nonstick skillet. Add half the batter to the pan in separate spoonfuls to make 6 small pancakes. Cook for 2–3 minutes on each side, until golden and cooked through. Set aside on paper towels while you cook the remaining batter.

Pile the pancakes onto serving plates and arrange the smoked salmon and mascarpone on top. Sprinkle with the chives and serve.

For corn & salmon pasta, cook 1 lb fresh penne according to the package directions until al dente. Add 1 cup frozen corn kernels for the last 1 minute of cooking. Drain and return to the pan. Stir in ⅓ cup crème fraîche or sour cream and 5 oz smoked salmon, torn into strips. Sprinkle with a handful of chives, chopped, to serve. **Total cooking time 10 minutes.**

hot potato blinis with beets

[handwritten: Quick]

Serves **4**

Total cooking time **30 minutes**

1 cup **cooked mashed potatoes** *[handwritten: 1 cup]*

⅓ cup plus 1 tablespoon **all-purpose flour**

½ teaspoon **baking powder**

3 **extra-large eggs**, separated

2 tablespoons **sour cream**

¼ cup finely chopped **dill**

vegetable oil, for frying

salt and **black pepper**

For the topping *[handwritten: can be prepared ahead of time]*

2 **cooked beets**, peeled and finely diced

⅓ cup **crème fraîche** or **sour cream**

1 tablespoon **creamed horseradish**

freshly ground black pepper

chopped **chives**, to garnish

Put the mashed potatoes into a bowl. Beat in the flour, baking powder, egg yolks, sour cream, and dill and season well.

Whisk the egg whites in a large, grease-free bowl until stiff. Using a metal spoon, carefully fold the beaten egg whites into the potato mixture.

Heat a little oil in a large, nonstick skillet, then add 3–4 separate tablespoons of the potato blini mixture. Cook over medium heat until set, then turn the potato blinis over and cook briefly so that both sides are lightly browned. Remove and keep warm in a low oven. Repeat the process until all the potato mixture has been used.

Meanwhile, mix together most of the beets, reserving a little to garnish, crème fraîche or sour cream, and creamed horseradish and season well.

Spoon the beet mixture over the blinis, then garnish with the reserved beets, chopped chives, and freshly ground black pepper.

For potato & chive soup, melt 2 tablespoons butter in a saucepan. When it begins to foam, add 1 diced onion and toss in the butter until well coated. Stir in 2 cups cooked mashed potatoes and 4 cups hot vegetable broth. Bring to a boil and add ½ cup milk. Puree the soup with an immersion blender. Season. Stir in 3 tablespoons each finely chopped dill and chives. Serve immediately with crusty bread. **Total cooking time 20 minutes.**

crayfish cocktail

No! (handwritten)

Serves **4**
Total cooking time **10 minutes**

⅓ cup **mayonnaise**
2 tablespoons **ketchup**
Tabasco sauce, to taste
lemon juice, to taste
12 oz **cooked peeled crayfish tails**
2 **small butterhead lettuce**, such as Boston lettuce, leaves separated
2 small **ripe avocado**, pitted, peeled, and sliced
salt and **black pepper**
paprika, to garnish

Mix together the mayonnaise and ketchup in a bowl, add Tabasco sauce and lemon juice to taste, and season. Stir through the crayfish.

Arrange the lettuce in serving dishes with the avocado slices. Spoon the crayfish mixture over them. Sprinkle with some paprika to garnish.

For Mexican-style seafood cocktail, put 5 oz raw, peeled shrimp into a bowl. Pour enough boiling water over them to cover and let stand for 2 minutes. Add 5 oz shelled and cleaned scallops, adding a little more boiling water, and let stand for an additional 3 minutes, then drain. Mix together 1¼ cups tomato juice, 1 tablespoon ketchup, a good squeeze of lime juice, and Tabasco sauce to taste. Stir together with the seafood and let stand for 10 minutes. Spoon into serving bowls. Top with 1 pitted, peeled, and chopped avocado, 1 sliced scallion, and a handful of chopped fresh cilantro. **Total cooking time 20 minutes.**

baked figs wrapped in prosciutto

Serves **4**

Total cooking time **20 minutes**

8 **figs**

4 oz **mozzarella cheese**,
  cut into 8 slices

8 slices of **prosciutto**

½ cup **olive oil**

2 tablespoons **balsamic
  vinegar**

4 cups **arugula**

salt and **black pepper**

Cut a deep cross into the top of each fig, nearly to the bottom, then place a slice of mozzarella inside. Wrap a slice of prosciutto around each fig. Brush the prosciutto with a little of the oil. Transfer to a baking sheet and cook in a preheated oven, at 425°F, for 7–10 minutes or until the ham is crisp and the cheese starts to melt.

Meanwhile, whisk the balsamic vinegar with the remaining oil and season well.

Toss most of the dressing with the arugula and arrange on plates. Add the baked figs and drizzle with a little more of the dressing. Serve immediately.

For fig & ham country salad, halve 8 figs and brush them with a little olive oil. Heat a ridged grill pan until smoking and then cook the cut sides of the figs for 1 minute, until lightly charred. Wrap each half in a slice of prosciutto. Mix 1 tablespoon finely chopped shallot with 1 tablespoon sherry vinegar and 3 tablespoons olive oil. Toss through 5 cups salad greens and serve with the grilled figs and some soft goat cheese crumbled on top. **Total cooking time 10 minutes.**

vietnamese spring rolls

Serves **4**

Total cooking time **30 minutes**

vegetable oil, for frying

4 oz lean **ground pork**

4 oz small **raw peeled shrimp**

¼ cup **cooked crabmeat**

1 **garlic clove**, crushed

1 teaspoon finely chopped **fresh ginger root**

2 **scallions**, finely chopped

1 tablespoon **soy sauce**

pinch of **sugar**

handful of ~~**fresh cilantro**~~, chopped

2 oz **dried fine rice noodles**

1 tablespoon **cornstarch**

1 tablespoon **water**

12 **spring roll wrappers**

salt and **black pepper**

To serve

chili sauce

herb salad (optional)

Heat 1 tablespoon oil in a wok or large skillet. Add the pork, shrimp, crabmeat, garlic, ginger, and scallions and stir-fry for 5 minutes, until just cooked through. Stir in the soy sauce and sugar and heat until bubbling, then stir in the cilantro and set aside to cool a little.

Meanwhile, prepare the noodles according to the directions on the package, then drain and add to the seafood mixture.

Mix the cornstarch with the measured water. Place a tablespoon of the seafood mixture on 1 spring roll wrapper. Brush the side with a little of the cornstarch mixture, then fold over and roll up. Repeat with the remaining seafood mixture and wrappers.

Fill a large, deep saucepan one-third full of oil and heat until a cube of bread browns in 15 seconds. Deep-fry the rolls, in batches, for 3 minutes, until golden and crisp, keeping the cooked rolls warm in a low oven. Drain on paper towels. Serve with chili sauce for dipping and a herb salad, if desired.

For Vietnamese summer rolls, prepare 2 oz dried fine rice noodles according to the directions on the package. Drain. Soften 12 rice paper wrappers in hot water for 30 seconds. Place on damp paper towels. Add some noodles to each wrapper along with 2 cooked peeled shrimp and some chopped lettuce, cored, seeded, and sliced red bell pepper, sliced carrot, ~~and chopped fresh cilantro~~. Moisten the edges, fold over, and roll up. Serve with chili sauce for dipping. **Total cooking time 20 minutes.**

baked mushrooms with taleggio

Serves **4**

Total cooking time **20 minutes**

8 large **flat mushrooms**, trimmed

8 slices of **Taleggio cheese**

¾ cup **dried bread crumbs**

1 **garlic clove**, crushed

⅓ cup **olive oil**

bunch of **basil leaves**, finely chopped

¼ cup finely grated **Parmesan cheese**

3 tablespoons **pine nuts**, toasted and chopped, plus extra to serve

salt and **black pepper**

Place the mushrooms, cap side down, on a baking sheet and top each one with a slice of Taleggio. Mix together the bread crumbs and garlic and sprinkle a little over each mushroom. Drizzle with some of the olive oil and bake in a preheated oven, at 400°F, for 15–20 minutes, until golden and crispy.

Meanwhile, mix together the basil, Parmesan cheese, pine nuts, and remaining oil and season.

Drizzle the pesto over the baked mushrooms and sprinkle with a few extra pine nuts to serve.

For baked leek & mushrooms, heat 2 tablespoons oil in a skillet, add 1 cleaned, trimmed, and thinly sliced leek and 4 oz trimmed and sliced mushrooms, and cook for 3–5 minutes, until softened. Meanwhile, whisk 6 eggs with ¼ cup heavy cream and a handful of chopped basil. Stir in the softened vegetables. Season and pour the mixture into a greased 8 inch square cake pan. Sprinkle with ¼ cup grated Parmesan cheese and bake in a preheated oven, at 350°F, for 25 minutes, until just set. **Total cooking time 30 minutes.**

celeriac remoulade with prosciutto

Serves **6**
Total cooking time **10 minutes**

⅓ cup **mayonnaise**
1 tablespoon **Dijon mustard**
2 tablespoons **crème fraîche**
   or **sour cream**
1 small **celeriac (celery root)**,
   peeled and cut into fine
   matchsticks
handful of **parsley**, finely
   chopped
6 slices of **prosciutto**
salt and **black pepper**

Mix together the mayonnaise, mustard, and crème fraîche or sour cream in a bowl until smooth. Season with salt and black pepper, add the celeriac (celery root) and parsley, and stir together.

Spoon the mixture onto serving plates along with the slices of prosciutto.

For celeriac remoulade & prosciutto rolls, whisk together 2 egg yolks and 1 teaspoon Dijon mustard, then slowly whisk in 1¼ cups olive oil, at first one drop at a time and then in a slow, steady stream, until creamy. Season with lemon juice and salt and black pepper. Stir through 1 tablespoon drained capers and a handful each of chopped parsley and chives. Peel ½ celeriac (celery root) and cut into thin matchsticks, then stir together with the mayonnaise. Spoon a little of the celeriac onto one end of a slice of prosciutto and roll up, repeating to make 12 rolls. Arrange them on a plate with some peppery leafy greens. **Total cooking time 20 minutes.**

tomato, shrimp & feta salad

Serves **4**
Total cooking time **30 minutes**

12 **cherry tomatoes**, halved
1/3 cup **olive oil**, plus extra
    for oiling
handful of **oregano leaves**,
    chopped
1 teaspoon crushed **fennel
    seeds**
1 tablespoon **balsamic
    vinegar**
5 oz large **cooked, peeled
    shrimp**, tails on
3 1/2 cups **arugula**
2 1/2 oz **feta cheese**, crumbled
    (about 1/2 cup)
salt and **black pepper**

Place the tomatoes, cut side up, on a lightly oiled
baking sheet. Drizzle with the oil, season with salt
and black pepper, then sprinkle a little of the
oregano and crushed fennel seeds over each tomato.
Place in a preheated oven, at 400°F, and cook for
15–20 minutes, until browned and slightly shriveled.
Let cool for a few minutes.

Toss the juices from the baking sheet with the
balsamic vinegar and shrimp. Arrange the shrimp
on a serving plate with the arugula and cooked
tomatoes. Sprinkle with the feta and serve.

For shrimp with sun-dried tomato feta dip, mash
together 1/3 cup cream cheese and 3 tablespoons
feta cheese until smooth, then thin with a little milk.
Stir in 3 drained and chopped sun-dried tomatoes in oil
and a handful of basil, chopped. Arrange 8 oz cooked
large, peeled shrimp on a serving plate and serve with
the dip. **Total cooking time 10 minutes.**

asparagus mimosa

Serves **4**

Total cooking time **20 minutes**

6 quail or 2 hen eggs

8 oz **asparagus spears**,
   trimmed

1 teaspoon **Dijon mustard**

1 tablespoon **white wine
   vinegar**

1 tablespoon **light cream**

⅓ cup **olive oil**

1 tablespoon drained **capers**

½ cup **pitted black ripe
   olives**, chopped

salt and **black pepper**

Bring a saucepan of water to a boil and gently lower
in the eggs. Cook the quail eggs for 5 minutes or the
hen eggs for 8 minutes. Remove from the pan and cool
under cold running water.

Meanwhile, cook the asparagus in a saucepan of
lightly salted boiling water for 3–5 minutes, until just
tender, drain, and cool under cold running water.

Stir together the mustard, vinegar, and cream and then
slowly whisk in the oil, a little at a time. Season well.

Arrange the asparagus on 4 plates and drizzle with
the dressing. Shell and coarsely chop the eggs, then
sprinkle with the asparagus together with the capers
and olives.

For asparagus tart, mix together 2 beaten eggs with
⅔ cup mascarpone cheese and ⅔ cup grated Parmesan
cheese. Place a sheet of ready-to-bake puff pastry
on a lightly greased baking sheet. Score a ½ inch
border around the pastry. Spread the egg mixture all
over the pastry inside the border, then arrange 8 oz
asparagus spears, trimmed, on top together with ¼ cup
coarsely chopped, pitted black ripe olives. Drizzle with
1 tablespoon olive oil and bake in a preheated oven,
at 400°F, for 15–20 minutes, until golden and puffed.
Total cooking time 30 minutes.

tarragon mushroom toasts

Serves 4
Total cooking time **20 minutes**

8 slices of **brioche**
1¼ sticks (5 oz) **butter**
2 **banana shallots**, finely
   chopped
3 **garlic cloves**, finely chopped
1 **red chile,** seeded and finely
   chopped (optional)
12 oz **mixed wild
   mushrooms**, such as
   chanterelle, porcini, and
   oyster, trimmed and sliced
¼ cup **crème fraîche** or
   sour cream, plus extra to
   garnish (optional)
2 tablespoons finely chopped
   tarragon
1 tablespoon finely chopped
   flat leaf parsley
salt and **black pepper**

Toast the brioche slices lightly and keep warm.

Heat the butter in a skillet and sauté the shallots, garlic, and chile, if using, for 1–2 minutes. Add the sliced mushrooms and sauté over medium heat for 6–8 minutes. Season well, remove from the heat, and stir in the crème fraîche or sour cream and chopped herbs.

Spoon the mushrooms onto the toasted brioche and serve immediately, with an extra dollop of crème fraîche or sour cream, if desired.

For chunky mushroom & tarragon soup, heat 2 (14½–15 oz) cans cream of mushroom soup in a saucepan along with 1 (16 oz) can whole button mushrooms. Bring to a boil, then reduce the heat and simmer for 2–3 minutes, until piping hot. Stir in ½ cup chopped tarragon and serve immediately, garnished with a little chopped flat leaf parsley. **Total cooking time 10 minutes.**

seasoned squid bites

Serves **4–6**
Total cooking time **20 minutes**

1 lb **cleaned squid**
2 teaspoons **black peppercorns**, crushed
1 teaspoon **dried red pepper flakes**
2 teaspoons **salt**
¾ cup **all-purpose flour**
vegetable oil, for deep-frying
2 **scallions**, cut into thick slices
1 **red chile**, cut into thick strips
lemon wedges, to serve

Cut each squid tube in half. Lay flat, inside up, and use a sharp knife to gently score across. Cut into bite-size pieces, then pat dry with paper towels.

Mix together the crushed peppercorns, red pepper flakes, salt, and flour in a bowl. Toss the squid in the seasoned mixture.

Fill a large, deep saucepan one-third full with oil and heat until a cube of bread browns in 15 seconds. Shake off the excess flour from a handful of squid and deep-fry for 2–3 minutes, until just golden and crisp. Drain on paper towels. Keep warm in a low oven. Repeat with the remaining squid.

Deep-fry the scallions and chile strips for 1–2 minutes, and use to garnish the squid. Serve with lemon wedges for squeezing over the squid.

For seasoned squid bites with chili relish, for the chili relish, put 2 large tomatoes into a saucepan with 1 cup sugar and 4 finely chopped red chiles. Add ¼ cup apple cider vinegar, 1 tablespoon Thai fish sauce, and a squeeze of lime juice. Bring to a boil, let the mixture bubble until the sugar melts, then simmer for 20 minutes, until sticky and thickened. Meanwhile, prepare and deep-fry the squid as above. Serve the squid hot with the chili relish. **Total cooking time 30 minutes.**

crab & mango salad

Serves **4**

Total cooking time **20 minutes**

¼ cup **sugar**

⅓ cup **water**

2 tablespoons **mirin**

1 **red chile**, sliced

1 **kaffir lime leaf**, shredded

finely grated zest and juice
    of 1 **lime**

1 **mango**, peeled, pitted,
    and chopped

3 oz **radishes**, halved

½ **cucumber**, sliced

1 (4 oz) bunch **watercress**
    or 4 cups **other peppery
    salad greens**

¾ cup **cooked fresh
    crabmeat**

Put the sugar, measured water, and mirin into a small saucepan, bring to a boil, and cook for 3 minutes, until it starts to turn syrupy. Stir in the chile, lime leaf, and lime zest and add lime juice to taste. Set aside for 5 minutes.

Toss together the mango, radishes, cucumber, and watercress or other salad greens and arrange on serving plates. Sprinkle the crabmeat on top and then drizzle with the dressing.

For wild rice, crab & mango salad, bring a large saucepan of lightly salted water to a boil, add 1 cup mixed wild and long-grain white rice, and cook for 25 minutes or according to the directions on the package, until just tender. Drain and rinse under cold running water to cool. Meanwhile, mix 1 tablespoon finely chopped red onion with 1 teaspoon finely chopped fresh ginger root, 1 finely chopped red chile, the finely grated zest and juice of 1 lime, and 3 tablespoons olive oil. Add the rice, a large handful of chopped fresh cilantro, 1 peeled, pitted, and chopped mango, and ⅔ cup cooked fresh crabmeat, stir well, and serve. **Total cooking time 30 minutes.**

moules marinières

Serves **4**
Total cooking time **15 minutes**

2 tablespoons **olive oil**
2 **garlic cloves**, sliced
3 lb **fresh mussels**, scrubbed
and debearded
1 cup **dry white wine**
handful of **flat leaf parsley**,
chopped
crusty bread, to serve

Heat the oil in a large saucepan. Add the garlic and cook for 30 seconds, until lightly golden. Add the mussels, discarding any that are cracked or don't shut when tapped, and the wine.

Cover the pan and cook for 5 minutes, shaking the pan occasionally, or until the mussels have opened. Discard any that remain closed.

Stir in the parsley, then serve with crusty bread.

For crispy baked mussels, heat 2 tablespoons olive oil in a large saucepan. Cook 2 sliced garlic cloves for 30 seconds, until lightly golden. Add 3 lb fresh mussels, scrubbed and debearded, discarding any that are cracked or don't shut when tapped, and 1 cup dry white wine, then season with salt. Cover and cook for 4 minutes, shaking the pan occasionally, until the mussels are just starting to open. Strain, reserving the liquid. Let cool a little, then discard any mussels that remain closed. Discard one half-shell from each mussel, leaving the mussels inside the remaining half-shells. Arrange on a baking sheet. Boil the reserved liquid until reduced to ¼ cup. Stir in ½ cup heavy cream and boil until reduced to ⅓ cup. Stir through a handful of flat leaf parsley, chopped. Spoon a little of the sauce over each mussel in its half-shell. Carefully sprinkle each mussel with some dried bread crumbs and top with a small pat of butter. Place in a preheated oven, at 425°F, for 5 minutes or until golden and bubbling. **Total cooking time 30 minutes.**

fava bean & anchovy salad

Serves **4**

Total cooking time **20 minutes**

7½ cups **fresh** or **frozen**
   fava beans (about 2½ lb)

3 tablespoons **olive oil**

3 cups **cherry tomatoes**,
   halved

6 **scallions**, sliced

2 **garlic cloves**, finely sliced

6 **anchovy fillets in oil**,
   drained and chopped

1 tablespoon shredded **basil**

1 tablespoon chopped **parsley**

2 cups **arugula**

2 tablespoons **Parmesan**
   cheese shavings, to serve

Blanch the fava beans in a saucepan of boiling water for 1 minute. Drain and refresh under cold running water. Peel off the outer skins.

Heat the olive oil in a skillet and cook the tomatoes over medium heat for 4–5 minutes.

Add the scallions and garlic and cook for an additional 1–2 minutes, then add the fava beans.

Stir in the anchovies and herbs and cook for another 1–2 minutes.

Spoon into a large serving bowl, toss with the arugula, and serve topped with the Parmesan shavings.

For roasted peppers with tomatoes & anchovies,

place 4 halved, cored, and seeded bell peppers, cut side up, in a roasting pan. Halve 8 tomatoes and divide among the bell peppers. Top each tomato half with 1–2 anchovy fillets, a few slices of garlic, and a few rosemary sprigs. Drizzle with 2–3 tablespoons olive oil, season with black pepper, and bake in a preheated oven, at 400°F, for 22–25 minutes. **Total cooking time 30 minutes.**

blue cheese soufflé

Serves **6**

Total cooking time **30 minutes**

3 slices of crustless
   sourdough bread,
   cut into chunks
1 cup **milk**
5 oz **blue cheese**, crumbled
   (about 1 cup)
4 tablespoons **butter**,
   softened, plus extra for
   greasing
4 **eggs**, separated
1 tablespoon **white wine
   vinegar**
3 tablespoons **olive oil**
1 teaspoon **walnut oil**
1 **crisp red apple**, cored
   and thinly sliced
handful of **arugula**
salt and **black pepper**

Put the bread into a bowl and pour the milk over it.
Let soak for 5 minutes, then squeeze any excess milk
from the bread. Transfer the bread to a food processor
or blender with the cheese, butter, and egg yolks and
blend until smooth. Season.

Whisk the egg whites in a large, grease-free bowl
until stiff peaks form. Stir a large spoonful into the
cheese mixture, then carefully fold in the remainder,
half at a time.

Spoon the mixture into six ¾-cup well-greased ramekins
or molds and bake in a preheated oven, at 425°F, for
10–15 minutes, until puffed and golden.

Meanwhile, whisk together the vinegar, olive oil, and
walnut oil and season. Toss together with the apple
and arugula.

Serve the soufflés immediately with the dressed
arugula and apple alongside.

For blue cheese Waldorf salad, mash 3 oz crumbled
blue cheese (about ⅔ cup) with ⅓ cup mayonnaise. Stir
together with 3 cored and chopped apples, 6 chopped
celery sticks, 2 sliced scallions, and ½ cup toasted,
chopped walnuts. Put into a serving dish and sprinkle
with some more walnuts, blue cheese, and celery leaves
to serve. **Total cooking time 10 minutes.**

pear, walnut & gorgonzola salad

Serves **4**
Total cooking time **10 minutes**

3 tablespoons **extra virgin
    olive oil**
1 teaspoon **Dijon mustard**
1 tablespoon **white wine
    vinegar**
1 teaspoon **sugar**
⅓ cup **walnut pieces**
1 **radicchio**, leaves separated
2 cups **arugula**
1 **romaine lettuce heart**,
    leaves separated and torn
2 **pears**, cored and sliced
6 oz **Gorgonzola cheese**
    or **other blue cheese**,
    crumbled (about 1¼ cups)

Whisk together the olive oil, mustard, vinegar, and sugar in a small bowl.

Toast the walnut pieces in a dry skillet until golden to help bring out their flavor.

Toss together the radicchio, arugula, and romaine leaves in a bowl. Divide the leaves among 4 plates and sprinkle with the slices of pear. Sprinkle with the Gorgonzola or other blue cheese and the walnuts.

Pour the dressing over the salad and serve.

For Gorgonzola with warm Marsala pears, place four 4 oz slices of Gorgonzola cheese or other blue cheese in a serving dish. Core and cut 2 pears into eighths. Heat 1 tablespoon olive oil in a skillet and cook the pears for 3–4 minutes on each side. Whisk together 2 tablespoons each honey and Marsala or a medium red wine, then pour into the pan, letting it simmer and thicken for a few minutes. Using a slotted spoon, remove the pears and place them on top of the blue cheese. Cook ½ cup walnut halves in the remaining syrup in the pan. Pour the syrup and walnuts over the pears and Gorgonzola to serve. **Total cooking time 20 minutes.**

cheese-stuffed onions

Serves **4**
Total cooking time **30 minutes**

4 large **onions**, peeled
1 tablespoon **olive oil**
½ bunch (5–6 oz) **spinach**,
    ends trimmed
½ cup **ricotta cheese**
1 **egg yolk**
1 teaspoon chopped **thyme**
1 oz **Fontina cheese**
½ cup grated **Parmesan**
    cheese
2 tablespoons **butter**

To serve
2 cups **arugula**
3 tablespoons **balsamic syrup**

Blanch the onions in boiling water for 5 minutes. Drain and let cool for 5 minutes.

Meanwhile, heat the oil in a large saucepan, add the spinach, and cook until wilted. Remove from the pan and coarsely chop. Place in a bowl with the ricotta, egg yolk, thyme, Fontina, and ¼ cup of the grated Parmesan.

Slice off the top of each onion and remove the middle sections with a fork.

Spoon the cheese mixture into the onions and place them in a roasting pan. Sprinkle with the remaining Parmesan, dot with the butter, and roast in a preheated oven, at 400°F, for 15 minutes, until the cheese is bubbling and golden.

Serve the stuffed onions on a bed of arugula, drizzled with the balsamic syrup.

For cheese & onion bruschetta, heat 1 tablespoon olive oil in a skillet and sauté 1 large sliced onion for 2–3 minutes, until soft. Stir in ½ teaspoon sugar and 1 teaspoon balsamic vinegar and cook for an additional 1–2 minutes. Toast 8 slices of ciabatta on both sides. Top each one with the caramelized onions and 4 oz crumbled Gorgonzola cheese or other blue cheese (about ¾ cup). Cook under a preheated hot broiler until the cheese is golden and bubbling. **Total cooking time 15 minutes.**

caesar salad

Serves **4**

Total cooking time **20 minutes**

½ **baguette**, torn into chunks

2 tablespoons **olive oil**

12 **quail eggs**

1 **garlic clove**, crushed

2 anchovy fillets in oil, drained and finely chopped

2 tablespoons **crème fraîche** or **sour cream**

1 teaspoon **Dijon mustard**

¼ cup **extra virgin olive oil**

¼ cup grated **Parmesan cheese**, plus extra shavings to serve

lemon juice, to taste

2 **baby romaine lettuce**, leaves separated

black pepper

Toss the baguette chunks with the olive oil, transfer to a baking sheet, and bake in a preheated oven, at 400°F, for 7–10 minutes, until golden and crisp. Let cool.

Meanwhile, bring a saucepan of water to a boil, gently lower in the eggs, and cook for 5 minutes. Remove from the pan and cool under cold running water. Shell and halve.

Mix together the garlic, anchovies, crème fraîche or sour cream, and mustard in a bowl, then slowly whisk in the extra virgin olive oil. Stir through the grated Parmesan, season with black pepper, and stir in lemon juice to taste.

Arrange the salad greens on plates along with the baguette chunks and eggs. Drizzle with the sauce and sprinkle with Parmesan shavings to serve.

For open chicken caesar sandwich, mash 1 drained anchovy fillet in oil and mix with ¼ cup mayonnaise, a handful of grated Parmesan cheese, and 1 tablespoon lemon juice. Spread the mixture over 4 slices of lightly toasted bread and top with 1 baby romaine lettuce, coarsely chopped. Place 2 sliced cooked chicken breasts on top and grate a little more Parmesan over the sandwiches. **Total cooking time 10 minutes.**

brie & thyme melts

Serves **4**

Total cooking time **10 minutes**

1 **ciabatta-style loaf**, cut in
   half horizontally
⅓ cup **onion relish**
7 oz **Brie** or **Camembert
   cheese**, sliced
1 teaspoon **dried thyme**
4 teaspoons **chile, garlic,
   or basil oil**
tomato salad, to serve
   (optional)

Cut the 2 pieces of bread in half to have 4 portions.
Arrange, cut side up, on a baking sheet and spread
each piece with the onion relish.

Lay the cheese slices on top and sprinkle with the
thyme. Drizzle with the flavored oil and cook under a
preheated hot broiler for 3–4 minutes, until the cheese
begins to melt. Serve immediately with a tomato salad,
if desired.

For whole baked cheese with garlic & thyme,

cut some little slits in the top of a whole 8 oz round
Camembert or baby Brie. Insert 1 thinly sliced garlic
clove and 5–6 small thyme sprigs into the slits. Drizzle
with 2 teaspoons chile, garlic, or basil oil, then wrap in
a loose aluminum foil package and bake in a preheated
oven, at 350°F, for about 15 minutes, until soft and
oozing. Serve with toasted ciabatta, onion relish, and
a tomato salad. **Total cooking time 20 minutes.**

meat & poultry

beef skewers with satay sauce

Serves **4**

Total cooking time **30 minutes**

12 oz **tenderloin** or **top sirloin steak**

⅓ cup **dark soy sauce**

2 tablespoons **sesame oil**

2 tablespoons **rice vinegar** or **mirin**

1 tablespoon packed **dark brown sugar**

1 inch piece of **fresh ginger root**, peeled and finely grated

1 **garlic clove**, crushed

crudites, such as carrot sticks, sugar snap peas, and cucumber sticks, to serve

For the sauce

⅓ cup **chunky peanut butter**

3 tablespoons **dark soy sauce**

1 small **red chile,** finely chopped

⅔ cup **boiling water**

Cut the steak into long, thin strips. Mix together the soy sauce, oil, vinegar or mirin, sugar, ginger, and garlic in a nonmetallic bowl. Add the steak and toss well to coat. Cover and let marinate for 15 minutes.

Meanwhile, heat all the ingredients for the sauce in a saucepan over gentle heat, stirring continuously with a wooden spoon, until smooth and thick. Transfer to a small serving bowl and place on a serving platter with the crudites.

Thread the beef onto 8 metal skewers, or bamboo skewers presoaked in cold water for 30 minutes, and cook under a preheated hot broiler for 2 minutes on each side, until browned and just cooked.

Transfer to the serving platter with the sauce and crudites and serve immediately.

For Asian-style teriyaki beef on lettuce platters, slice 12 oz trimmed tenderloin steak into thin slices and mix with 2 tablespoons prepared teriyaki marinade in a bowl. In a separate bowl, mix ½ cucumber, diced, with 2 tablespoons chopped fresh cilantro, 1 teaspoon dried red pepper flakes, and the juice of 1 lime. Heat 1 teaspoon vegetable oil in a large skillet and cook the steak over high heat for 1 minute on each side. Pile the cucumber mixture into 8 small butterhead lettuce leaves, top with the beef, and sprinkle with chopped scallions. **Total cooking time 15 minutes.**

beef carpaccio & bean salad

Serves **4**
Total cooking time **30 minutes**

8 oz **beef tenderloin** or
  filet mignon
3 tablespoons **extra virgin
  olive oil**
1 teaspoon **freshly ground
  black pepper**
1 tablespoon chopped **thyme**
1 teaspoon **Dijon mustard**
½ tablespoon **balsamic
  vinegar**
½ teaspoon honey
4 oz **green beans**, ends
  trimmed (about 1¼ cups)
1 (15 oz) can **cannellini
  (white kidney) beans**,
  rinsed and drained
1 **red onion**, finely sliced
1 oz **Parmesan cheese**
  shavings, to garnish

Place the beef on a cutting board and rub with 1 tablespoon of the oil, the black pepper, and thyme. Wrap in plastic wrap and put into the freezer for 20 minutes.

Meanwhile, whisk together the remaining oil with the mustard, vinegar, and honey to make a dressing.

Blanch the green beans for 2–3 minutes in boiling water, then drain and refresh under cold running water. Toss the green beans, cannellini (white kidney) beans, and onion in the dressing and let stand at room temperature until the beef finishes chilling.

Unwrap the beef, slice as thinly as possible, and arrange on a platter. Spoon the bean salad over the meat, along with all the dressing, and garnish with Parmesan shavings.

For quick beef carpaccio & bean salad, whisk together 3 tablespoons olive oil, 1 tablespoon balsamic vinegar, 1 teaspoon mustard, and 1 teaspoon honey. Blanch 4 oz trimmed green beans (about 1¼ cups) for 2–3 minutes in boiling water, then drain and refresh under cold running water. Toss in the dressing with 1 (15 oz) can cannellini (white kidney) beans, rinsed and drained, and let stand at room temperature while preparing the beef. Arrange 8 oz store-bought thinly sliced beef carpaccio on a platter, spoon the bean salad over the meat, and garnish with Parmesan shavings. **Total cooking time 15 minutes.**

hoisin chicken pancakes

Serves **4**

Total cooking time **20 minutes**

1 tablespoon **vegetable oil**

3 **boneless, skinless chicken breasts** (about 5 oz each), cut into strips

2 tablespoons **hoisin sauce**, plus extra for dipping

½ teaspoon **ginger paste**

2 teaspoons **dark soy sauce**

8 **thin rice flour pancakes** (available at Asian supermarkets, or make from a gluten-free pancake mix, adding extra liquid for a crepe-like thin pancake)

1 cup **bean sprouts**, blanched in boiling water for 30 seconds, drained, and refreshed under cold running water

4 **scallions**, cut into thin strips

½ **cucumber**, cut into thin strips

Heat the oil in a wok or skillet, add the chicken, and cook over high heat for 5 minutes or until cooked through. Add the hoisin sauce, ginger paste, and soy sauce and cook, stirring, until the sauce is sticky and coats the chicken. Remove from the heat.

Warm the pancakes in a microwave oven or in a low oven according to the directions on the package.

Divide the bean sprouts, scallions, and cucumber among the pancakes, top with the chicken, and roll up. Serve with extra hoisin sauce for dipping.

For hoisin chicken packages, in a large bowl, mix together 2 tablespoons hoisin sauce, ½ teaspoon ginger paste, and 2 teaspoons dark soy sauce. Add 2 boneless, skinless chicken breasts (about 6 oz each), thinly sliced, 4 scallions, cut into strips, 1 cup bean sprouts, and 1 large carrot, cut into strips. Divide the mixture among 4 large squares of double-thickness parchment paper. Fold the paper over the filling, twisting the edges to form a package. Place on a baking sheet and cook in a preheated oven, at 400°F, for 20 minutes. Serve with freshly cooked noodles. **Total cooking time 30 minutes.**

smoked duck citrus salad

Serves **4**

Total cooking time **15 minutes**

2 **clementines**

1 (4 oz) bunch **watercress**
   or 4 cups **other peppery
   salad greens**

½ cup **walnuts**, lightly crushed

8 oz **smoked duck breast**,
   sliced

To garnish (optional)

micro leaves or **alfalfa
   sprouts**

pomegranate seeds

For the dressing

2 tablespoons **walnut oil**

2 teaspoons **raspberry
   vinegar**

salt and **black pepper**

Cut away the peel and pith from the clementines. Cut the flesh into segments, discarding the membrane, but reserving the juice in a small bowl.

Arrange the watercress or other salad greens on 4 plates and sprinkle with the clementine segments and the walnuts. Top with the smoked duck slices and garnish with the micro leaves or alfalfa sprouts and pomegranate seeds, if desired.

Whisk the oil and vinegar for the dressing into the reserved clementine juice and season. Drizzle the dressing over the salad and serve.

For warm duck, clementine & walnut salad, prepare the clementines and dressing following the recipe above. Put 2 tablespoons olive oil into a skillet over medium heat. Generously season 6 oz duck breast strips and sprinkle with ½ teaspoon Sichuan pepper. Place in the hot pan and cook for 3–4 minutes, turning once, until cooked but still slightly pink. Transfer to a warm place to rest for 10 minutes. Slice the duck strips and sprinkle with the clementine segments, ½ cup lightly crushed walnuts, and a handful of pomegranate seeds. Serve drizzled with the dressing. **Total cooking time 25 minutes.**

chicken satay

12 **prepared chicken satay skewers**

3 cups **cooked Thai rice** or 2 (9 oz) packages **precooked rice**

¼ cup **mayonnaise**

2 tablespoons **chunky peanut butter**

1 teaspoon **Thai red curry paste**

2 **scallions**, sliced

Reheat the chicken satay skewers in a microwave oven or in a hot skillet for 2–3 minutes.

Meanwhile, reheat the rice in a microwave oven or saucepan until steaming hot, or follow the directions on the packages.

Mix together the mayonnaise, peanut butter, and Thai curry paste and pour into a small serving bowl.

Serve the chicken skewers with the rice and sauce, with the scallions sprinkled over the top.

For chicken satay skewers, cut 4 boneless, skinless chicken breasts (about 5 oz each), into strips and coat in a mixture of 1 tablespoon dark soy sauce, 1 teaspoon packed dark brown sugar, 1 teaspoon lemon grass paste, and 1 teaspoon Thai red curry paste. Let marinate for 10 minutes. Thread the chicken, concertina style, onto metal or bamboo skewers presoaked in cold water for 30 minutes and place them on an aluminum foil-lined broiler pan. Cook under a preheated hot broiler for 5 minutes, until cooked through. Meanwhile, make a peanut dipping sauce. Warm 2 tablespoons chunky peanut butter with 1 teaspoon Thai red curry paste and ¼ cup coconut milk in a small saucepan. Serve the chicken skewers with the peanut sauce separately and a crisp salad. **Total cooking time 30 minutes.**

tuscan-style tarts

Serves **4**
Total cooking time **20 minutes**

1 sheet **ready-to-bake puff pastry**
2 **tomatoes**, sliced
1 cup **spicy tomato-flavored chicken slices**
8 small pieces of **roasted red pepper** from a jar, drained
1 tablespoon ~~thyme leaves~~
1 cup **Kalamata olives**
1 tablespoon **olive oil**
salt and **black pepper**
green salad, to serve

Place the pastry onto a work surface and cut out four 5 inch circles. Place the circles, well spaced apart, on a large baking sheet. Prick them all over with a fork.

Arrange the tomato slices randomly on top of each one, dividing them evenly among the tart shells and keeping a ½ inch border around the edge. Divide the chicken slices, roasted peppers, ~~thyme~~, and olives evenly among the tart shells, then drizzle with the olive oil and season.

Bake at the top of a preheated oven, at 425˚F, for 12–15 minutes or until the pastry is puffed and golden and the topping soft. Serve the tarts with a simple green salad.

For Tuscan tart with artichokes & lemon, place a sheet of ready-to-bake puff pastry on a large baking sheet. Sprinkle with 1 (14 oz) well-drained jar of artichokes mixed with the finely grated zest of 1 lemon and ¼ cup chopped parsley. Toss 1 cup cooked spicy tomato chicken slices with 1 tablespoon of the artichoke oil or olive oil and sprinkle over the top with 1 chopped tomato and 1 cup Kalamata olives. Bake in a preheated oven, at 425˚F, for 25 minutes or until well puffed and golden. **Total cooking time 30 minutes.**

ginger & cilantro turkey burgers

Serves **4**

Total cooking time **20 minutes**

1 lb **ground turkey**
1 tablespoon finely grated
   fresh ginger root
3 tablespoons finely chopped
   fresh cilantro
1 cup **fresh white**
   bread crumbs
2 teaspoons **dark soy sauce**
2 tablespoons lightly
   beaten **egg**
2 tablespoons **vegetable oil**
black pepper

To serve
¼ cup **chili relish**
4 large or 8 small **bread rolls**,
   halved and grilled
4–8 **lettuce leaves**

Put the turkey into a large bowl with the ginger, cilantro, bread crumbs, and soy sauce. Season with black pepper and add the egg, mixing well to combine. Form into 4 large or 8 small patties.

Heat the oil in a large, nonstick skillet and cook the patties for 3–4 minutes on each side, until cooked through and golden.

Spread the chili relish onto the bottom halves of the grilled rolls and top with the lettuce leaves. Place a burger on top of each and cover with the top half. Serve immediately.

For baked turkey breast with ginger & cilantro, mix together 1 tablespoon finely grated fresh ginger root, 3 tablespoons finely chopped fresh cilantro, 2 tablespoons chili relish, and 1 tablespoon light soy sauce in a bowl. Cut some slashes in 4 turkey breast cutlets (about 5 oz each), and massage in the ginger and cilantro marinade. Put into an ovenproof dish and cover with aluminum foil. Cook in a preheated oven, at 400°F, for about 20 minutes, until cooked through. Serve with 3 cups cooked rice, extra chili relish, and lime wedges. **Total cooking time 30 minutes.**

stir-fried duck with orange rice

Serves **4**
Total cooking time **20 minutes**

1 cup **instant long-grain rice**
2 tablespoons **sesame oil**
1 **red onion**, cut into slim
  wedges
4 **boneless, skin-on duck
  breasts** (about 5 oz each),
  thickly sliced
1 bunch of **scallions**, cut into
  1 inch lengths
3 cups **sugar snap peas**
finely pared zest and juice of
  1 orange
2 tablespoons **dark soy sauce**
1 tablespoon packed
  light brown sugar
salt

Bring a large saucepan of lightly salted water to a boil and cook the rice according to the package directions until tender. Drain, if necessary, and keep warm.

Meanwhile, heat the oil in a large wok or heavy skillet over medium-high heat and stir-fry the red onion for 5 minutes. Add the duck slices and stir-fry for 5 minutes, until the duck is almost cooked. Add the scallions and sugar snap peas and stir-fry over high heat for 2 minutes.

Add the drained rice to the pan and toss well. Mix together the orange zest and juice, soy sauce, and sugar in a small bowl, then pour the sauce over the duck mixture and toss well to distribute it through the dish. Serve immediately in warm serving bowls.

For Chinese duck noodles, heat 2 tablespoons sesame oil in a large wok or heavy skillet over medium-high heat and stir-fry 4 boneless, skin-on duck breasts (about 5 oz each), thickly sliced, for 5 minutes. Add 1 bunch of scallions, cut into 1 inch lengths, and 3 cups sugar snap peas and stir-fry over high heat for 2 minutes. Stir in 12 oz cooked rice noodles and ⅓ cup hoisin sauce and heat through for 2 minutes. **Total cooking time 15 minutes.**

butter & lemon-roasted chicken

Serves **4**
Total cooking time **30 minutes**

8 **boneless, skinless chicken thighs**
finely grated zest and juice of 1 **lemon**
3 tablespoons chopped **parsley**
4 tablespoons **butter**
black pepper
seasonal vegetables, to serve

Open out the chicken thighs, then put them in a large bowl with the lemon zest and juice, parsley, and plenty of black pepper. Mix well to coat the chicken. Roll each of the coated thighs back into shape and secure with a toothpick.

Put the chicken thighs into a roasting pan, pouring any remaining juices over them, and top each with a small pat of butter. Cook in a preheated oven, at 400°F, for 20–25 minutes or until golden and cooked through. Serve with seasonal vegetables.

For pan-fried thighs with lemon & butter, open out 8 boneless, skinless chicken thighs and cut in half along each width. Place the chicken pieces in a large bowl with the finely grated zest and juice of 1 lemon and 3 tablespoons chopped parsley. Season with salt and black pepper and mix well. Heat 4 tablespoons butter in a large, heavy skillet and cook the chicken, turning frequently, for 15 minutes or until golden and cooked through. Serve with instant mashed potatoes or rice. **Total cooking time 20 minutes.**

quick paella

Serves **4**
Total cooking time **30 minutes**

2 tablespoons **olive oil**
4 **chicken drumsticks**
3 oz **chorizo sausage**,
   thinly sliced
1 small **red onion**, thinly sliced
1 cup **Spanish rice**
   or **risotto rice**
4 cups **rich chicken broth**
pinch of **saffron threads**
1 (14 oz) can **artichoke**
   hearts, drained and halved
4 oz large **peeled shrimp**
4 oz **green beans**, ends
   trimmed (about **1** cup)

Heat the oil in a large paella pan, wok, or skillet
and cook the chicken drumsticks, turning occasionally,
over high heat for 5 minutes or until browned. Add
the chorizo and onion to the pan and cook, stirring,
for 2 minutes.

Add the rice and toss to mix. Pour in all the broth
and the saffron threads, then bring to a boil. Reduce
the heat, cover, and simmer, stirring occasionally, for
15 minutes or according to the directions on the
package of rice.

Stir in the artichokes, shrimp, and beans. Cook, covered,
for an additional 5 minutes, until all the ingredients are
piping hot, cooked through, and tender.

For chicken, shrimp & chorizo pilaf, cook 1¼ cups
instant white rice in a large saucepan of lightly salted
boiling water according to the package directions until
tender, then drain. Meanwhile, heat 3 tablespoons
olive oil in a large skillet and cook 1 sliced red onion
and 8 oz diced chicken meat with 3 oz sliced chorizo
sausage for 8–10 minutes or until browned. Add
1 (14 oz) can artichokes, drained and halved, ⅔ cup
frozen peas, and ⅔ cup chicken broth. Bring to a boil
and cook for 2 minutes. Add the drained rice and toss
together. Serve in warm serving bowls with chopped
parsley to garnish, if desired. **Total cooking time
20 minutes.**

corn-crusted pork

Serves **4**
Total cooking time **30 minutes**

¼ cup **instant grits**
¼ cup grated **Parmesan cheese**
2 tablespoons **all-purpose flour**
1 **egg**, beaten
4 **pork cutlets** (about 5 oz each)
3 **pears**, cored and sliced
1 **red onion**, sliced
3 cups **arugula**
2 tablespoons **walnut pieces**
3 tablespoons **olive oil**
1 tablespoon **balsamic vinegar**
4 tablespoons **butter**

Mix together the grits and Parmesan in a shallow bowl. Put the flour and egg into separate bowls.

Dip the pork into the flour and then the egg, followed by the grits mixture. Chill for 5 minutes.

Put the pears, onion, arugula, and walnuts into a bowl and toss with 2 tablespoons of the olive oil and the balsamic vinegar.

Heat the remaining oil and butter in a skillet and cook the pork cutlets for 3–4 minutes on each side, until browned and cooked through.

Serve on a bed of the dressed salad.

For pork cutlets with pears, heat 2 tablespoons olive oil in a roasting pan on the stove and cook 2 red onions, cut into wedges, 2 cored and quartered pears, and a few sprigs of rosemary for about 10 minutes, until the onions and pears are softened and well browned. Add 4 pork cutlets (about 5 oz each) and cook for 2–3 minutes on each side, until cooked through. Add 2–3 oz Gorgonzola cheese, crumbled over the top, and place the roasting pan under a preheated hot broiler. Cook until the cheese starts to melt. Serve with steamed green vegetables. **Total cooking time 25 minutes.**

baked lamb-stuffed eggplant

Serves **4**

Total cooking time **30 minutes**

5 tablespoons **olive** or
   vegetable oil
2 **small eggplants**,
   halved lengthwise
1 **onion**, chopped
2 **garlic cloves**, sliced
3 tablespoons **pine nuts**
12 oz **ground lamb**
2 teaspoons **ground cumin**
½ teaspoon **ground
   cinnamon**
3 tablespoons chopped **mint**
⅓ cup **dry white wine**
3½ oz **feta cheese**, crumbled
   (about ⅔ cup)
salt and **black pepper**

To serve
steamed **couscous**
lemon wedges

Heat 3 tablespoons of the oil in a roasting pan on the stove and cook the eggplants, cut sides down, for 5 minutes, until browned, then turn and cook the other side for 2–3 minutes. Season generously and transfer, cut sides up, to a preheated oven, at 400°F, for 8–10 minutes.

Meanwhile, heat the remaining oil in a large skillet. Add the onion and garlic and cook for 5–6 minutes. Add the pine nuts and cook for 1–2 minutes, until golden.

Add the ground lamb to the pan with the cumin and cinnamon and cook over medium-high heat, stirring frequently, for 5–6 minutes, until browned. Stir in the chopped mint and season lightly.

Remove the eggplants from the oven, spoon the lamb mixture over the top, and pour the white wine over the meat. Sprinkle the feta over the top and return to the oven for an additional 10 minutes, until bubbling and lightly browned. Serve with lemon wedges and steamed couscous.

For grilled lamb with pine nuts, mix ⅓ cup olive oil with 2 teaspoons ground cumin, ½ teaspoon ground cinnamon, grated zest of 1 lemon, and salt and black pepper, and rub into 4 lamb cutlets (about 4 oz each). Heat a ridged grill pan and cook the lamb cutlets for 3–4 minutes on each side. Sprinkle with 3 tablespoons pine nuts, 3 tablespoons chopped mint, and 3½ oz crumbled feta cheese (⅔ cup), and serve with couscous and lemon wedges. **Total cooking time 10 minutes.**

pork chops with plum relish

Serves **4**

Total cooking time **20 minutes**

2 tablespoons **olive oil**

1 small **onion**, finely chopped

1 tablespoon grated **fresh ginger root**

4 **plums**, pitted and sliced

1 tablespoon packed **light brown sugar**

1 teaspoon **red wine vinegar**

finely grated zest of ½ **orange**

½ cup **water**

4 **pork chops** (about 5 oz each)

salt and **black pepper**

handful of **peppery salad greens**, to serve

Heat 1 tablespoon of the oil in a small saucepan, add the onion, and cook for 5 minutes, until softened. Add the ginger, plums, sugar, vinegar, orange zest, and measured water and simmer for 10 minutes, until soft. Season.

Meanwhile, rub the remaining oil over the chops and season. Cook under a preheated hot broiler for 5 minutes on each side until just cooked through.

Serve with spoonfuls of the relish and the watercress.

For broiled pork with plum salsa, rub 1 tablespoon olive oil over 4 pork chops (about 5 oz each). Season and cook under a preheated hot broiler for 5 minutes on each side, until browned and cooked through. Meanwhile, pit and coarsely chop 3 plums and put into a small bowl. Add 1 finely chopped red chile, the juice of ½ lime, 1 tablespoon orange juice, and 2 tablespoons olive oil. Mix together and spoon the salsa over the pork chops to serve. **Total cooking time 15 minutes.**

warm tomato, liver & bacon salad

Serves **4**

Total cooking time **15 minutes**

2 tablespoons **olive oil**
4 oz **smoked bacon**, chopped
8 oz **chicken livers**, trimmed
4 **ripe tomatoes**, sliced
4 cups **mâche** or **corn salad**
½ **red onion**, halved and
   sliced
salt and **black pepper**

For the dressing
3 tablespoons **olive oil**
1 tablespoon **red wine**
   vinegar
1 teaspoon **Dijon mustard**
pinch of **sugar**

Heat the oil in a nonstick skillet and cook the bacon for 3–4 minutes, until crisp and browned. Remove from the pan with a slotted spoon and set aside. Season the chicken livers with salt and black pepper and add to the hot pan. Cook for 4–5 minutes, until browned and cooked through.

Meanwhile, combine all the dressing ingredients in a screw-top jar with a tight-fitting lid and shake well.

Arrange the tomatoes on 4 plates with the mâche or corn salad and onion. Sprinkle the liver and bacon over the prepared salads and serve immediately, drizzled with the dressing.

For liver & bacon tagliatelle, heat 2 tablespoons olive oil in a skillet and cook 4 oz chopped smoked bacon for 3–4 minutes. Add 1 chopped red onion and 2 chopped garlic cloves. Cook for 4–5 minutes. Meanwhile, cook 1 lb dried tagliatelle according to the package directions until al dente. Add 8 oz chicken livers, trimmed, to the skillet and cook for 2–3 minutes to brown, then add 2 tablespoons dry sherry, scraping the bottom of the pan to loosen any sediment. Add 1 cup light cream, 4 drained and chopped sun-dried tomatoes in oil, and 1 teaspoon dried sage. Season and simmer for 2–3 minutes, until the livers are just cooked. When ready, drain the tagliatelle and serve with the liver and bacon. **Total cooking time 20 minutes.**

steak with peppercorn sauce

Serves **4**

Total cooking time **10 minutes**

2 tablespoons **olive oil**

4 **hanger steaks** or **skirt steaks** (about 4 oz each)

2 tablespoons **butter**

½ cup **light cream**

2 teaspoons **green peppercorns in liquid**, drained

salt and **black pepper**

To serve

green salad

fries or **crusty bread**

Heat the oil in a large, nonstick skillet and cook the steaks for 1–3 minutes on each side, depending on how you prefer your steak. Season with salt and black pepper, remove the steaks from the pan, and transfer to a warm ovenproof dish to rest.

Add the butter, cream, and peppercorns to the pan, and simmer over medium-low heat for 1–2 minutes, scraping the pan to loosen any tasty sediment.

Serve the steaks drizzled with the sauce, accompanied by green salad and fries or bread.

For green peppercorn burgers with blue cheese sauce, put 1 lb ground beef into a bowl with 1 chopped red onion, 2 teaspoons drained green peppercorns in liquid, ½ cup dried bread crumbs, 1 beaten egg, and 1 tablespoon finely chopped parsley or chives, then season and mix to combine. Form into 4 patties. Heat 2 tablespoons olive oil in a skillet and cook the patties for 4–5 minutes on each side, until cooked through. Meanwhile, put 4 oz creamy blue cheese (about ¾ cup) into a small bowl with 2 tablespoons crème fraîche or sour cream and plenty of black pepper. Mash together until smooth. Serve on buns with the burgers and some slices of fresh tomato. **Total cooking time 20 minutes.**

broiled tandoori lamb chops

Serves **4**

Total cooking time **20 minutes**

8 **lamb chops** or **lamb cutlets**
   (3–4 oz each)
3 **garlic cloves**, finely grated
1 teaspoon finely grated **fresh
   ginger root**
juice of 2 large **lemons**
1 tablespoon **ground cumin**
3 tablespoons **tandoori curry
   paste**
1 cup **plain yogurt**
vegetable oil, for oiling
salt and **black pepper**
chopped **mint leaves**,
   to garnish

To serve
cucumber salad
mini naans or **flatbreads**

Put the lamb into a single layer in a shallow, nonmetallic dish. Mix together the remaining ingredients, except the oil, in a bowl, then season well. Pour the mixture over the lamb, toss to coat evenly, then cover and let marinate for 10 minutes.

Place the lamb on a lightly oiled broiler rack and cook under a preheated hot broiler for 2–3 minutes on each side or until cooked to your preference.

Transfer to 4 warm serving plates, sprinkle with chopped mint, and serve with cucumber salad and mini naans or flatbreads.

For tandoori roasted rack of lamb, mix together 3 tablespoons tandoori curry paste and ½ cup Greek yogurt in a bowl. Using a small, sharp knife, make deep slashes in the meat of 2 French racks of lamb (with 7–8 ribs each). Season well, then spread the tandoori mixture all over the lamb. Put the racks, rib side up, on a nonstick baking sheet and put into a preheated oven, at 350°F, for 15–20 minutes or until cooked to your preference. Cover with aluminum foil and let rest for a few minutes before serving. **Total cooking time 30 minutes.**

beef & peppercorn stroganoff

Serves **4**
Total cooking time **15 minutes**

2 tablespoons **butter**
1 **red onion**, thinly sliced
8 oz **button mushrooms**,
   halved
3 tablespoons **tomato paste**
2 teaspoons **Dijon mustard**
1 tablespoon **pink
   peppercorns in liquid**,
   drained
1 tablespoon **green
   peppercorns in liquid**,
   drained
1 teaspoon **smoked paprika**
1¼ cups hot **beef broth**
1 lb **beef tenderloin**, cut into
   thin strips
1 cup **sour cream**
salt and **black pepper**
2 tablespoons chopped **flat
   leaf parsley**, to garnish
steamed **rice**, to serve

Heat a skillet until hot, then add half the butter. When foaming, add the red onion and sauté for 2–3 minutes or until just softened. Add the mushrooms, tomato paste, mustard, pink and green peppercorns, and paprika and cook, stirring, for an additional 1–2 minutes. Pour in the hot broth and bring to a boil, then reduce the heat to low and simmer for 1–2 minutes.

Meanwhile, heat a separate skillet and add the remaining butter. Season the beef. When the butter is foaming, add the beef and cook, stirring, for 2–3 minutes or until browned all over.

Add the sour cream and beef to the onion and mushroom mixture and mix well, then season.

Spoon into warm bowls, sprinkle with the parsley, and serve with steamed rice.

For quick beef & mushroom casseroles, use the cooked beef and mushroom mixture from the above recipe to fill 4 individual pie dishes. Top each with 1 cup cooked mashed potatoes and place under a hot broiler for 3–4 minutes or until golden. Serve with a salad. **Total cooking time 25 minutes.**

lamb cutlets with mashed peas

Serves **4**

Total cooking time **20 minutes**

6 **russet potatoes** (about
   1½ lb), peeled and chopped
2 cups **fresh** or **frozen peas**
1 tablespoon chopped
   rosemary
8 **lamb cutlets** (3–4 oz each)
2 tablespoons **butter**
salt and **black pepper**

Cook the potatoes in a saucepan of boiling water for 12–15 minutes, until tender, adding the peas 2 minutes before the end of the cooking time.

Meanwhile, sprinkle half the rosemary over the lamb cutlets, then cook them under a preheated hot broiler for 3–4 minutes on each side or until cooked to your preference. Let rest.

Drain the potatoes and peas, then return to the pan and lightly mash with the remaining rosemary, butter, and salt and black pepper to taste. Serve the lamb cutlets accompanied by the mashed peas.

For lamb racks with rosemary & garlic, cut small slits into four 3-cutlet racks of lamb and insert 2 sliced garlic cloves and 4 rosemary sprigs into the slits. Whisk together 1 tablespoon honey, 2 tablespoons whole-grain mustard, and 1 tablespoon prepared mint sauce in a bowl, then brush over the lamb. Let marinate at room temperature for 10 minutes. Place in a roasting pan and cook in a preheated oven, at 400°F, for 18 minutes or until cooked to your preference, basting with the marinade 2 or 3 times. Serve the lamb with grilled asparagus and mashed potatoes. **Total cooking time 30 minutes.**

creamy veal cutlets

Serves **4**
Total cooking time **30 minutes**

½ oz **dried porcini**
4 **veal cutlets** (about
    5 oz each)
2 tablespoons **all-purpose
    flour**
4 tablespoons **butter**
1 tablespoon **olive oil**
2 **garlic cloves**, chopped
1 **onion**, chopped
4 oz **cremini mushrooms**,
    trimmed and sliced
½ cup **white wine**
1 cup **light cream**
large handful of **baby spinach**
salt and **black pepper**
mashed potatoes, to serve

Soak the porcini in just enough boiling water to cover for 10 minutes. Drain, reserving the liquid, and coarsely chop the porcini.

Dust the veal cutlets with the flour. Heat the butter and the olive oil in a skillet and cook the cutlets for 2–3 minutes on each side, until just cooked through. Remove from the pan and keep warm.

Add the garlic, onion, and cremini mushrooms to the pan and sauté for 4–5 minutes, until the onion is soft.

Pour in the wine and simmer for 2–3 minutes, then pour in the cream and 2–3 tablespoons of the reserved porcini liquid.

Bring to a boil, then stir in the porcini and spinach and season with salt and black pepper. Return the cutlets to the pan and cook for 1 minute before serving with mashed potatoes.

For veal salad, heat 1 tablespoon olive oil in a skillet and cook 1 (10 oz) veal cutlet for 1–2 minutes on each side or until cooked to your preference. Let rest for 1–2 minutes, then slice thinly against the grain. In a large salad bowl, toss the veal with 2 chopped beefsteak tomatoes, 2 cups mixed salad greens, 1 cup arugula, 2 tablespoons chopped walnuts, and ½ cup drained and sliced roasted red peppers from a jar. Serve dressed with 2–3 tablespoons Italian salad dressing and sprinkled with 3 tablespoons Parmesan cheese shavings. **Total cooking time 15 minutes.**

harissa beef fajitas

Serves **4**
Total cooking time **15 minutes**

1 tablespoon **harissa paste**
½ teaspoon **paprika**
2 tablespoons **olive oil**
1 lb **sirloin steak**, cut into
   thick strips
8 **tortilla wraps**
½ **iceburg lettuce**, shredded
¼ cup **sour cream**
¼ cup **store-bought**
   guacamole
¼ cup **store-bought**
   tomato salsa
¼ cup shredded
   cheddar cheese

Mix together the harissa, paprika, and oil in a nonmetallic bowl. Add the steak and mix to coat, then cover and let marinate for 5 minutes.

Heat a ridged grill pan until hot, add the steak, and cook for 20 seconds on each side or until cooked to your preference. Remove from the pan and keep warm.

Warm the tortillas in a microwave oven according to the directions on the package. Sprinkle some shredded lettuce in the center of each tortilla and layer the steak on top. Spoon a little sour cream, guacamole, and salsa over the steak, then sprinkle the cheese over the top. Roll up the wraps and serve.

For harissa hamburgers, put 1 lb ground beef, 2 tablespoons chopped fresh cilantro, 1 tablespoon harissa paste, 1 chopped onion, 1 egg yolk, 1 tablespoon olive oil, and salt and black pepper into a food processor and process together. Shape the mixture into 4 equal patties, cover, and chill for 10 minutes. Cook the patties under a preheated medium broiler for 15 minutes, turning once. Meanwhile, toast 4 halved hamburger buns. Place a burger on each botttom and top with shredded iceburg lettuce, sliced tomatoes, sliced red onion, and a dollop of mayonnaise or sour cream. Top with the lids and serve. **Total cooking time 30 minutes.**

lamb & olive stew

Serves **4**

Total cooking time **30 minutes**

1 lb **boneless shoulder of lamb**, cut into small cubes

2 tablespoons **all-purpose flour**, seasoned

2 tablespoons **olive oil**

1 **onion**, chopped

2 **carrots**, peeled and diced

2 **garlic cloves**, chopped

1½ teaspoons chopped **rosemary**

1 cup **white wine**

1 (14½ oz) can **diced tomatoes**

12 **black ripe olives**, pitted

grated zest and juice of 1 **lemon**

2 tablespoons chopped **parsley**

4 cups **water**

1½ cups **instant grits**

2 tablespoons **butter**

2 tablespoons grated **Parmesan cheese**

Dust the cubes of lamb with the seasoned flour. Heat the olive oil in a saucepan and brown the meat all over.

Add the onion and cook for 3 minutes, stirring, then add the carrots, garlic, and rosemary and cook for an additional 3–4 minutes, until the vegetables are softened.

Pour in the white wine and diced tomatoes, bring to a boil, then simmer for 20 minutes, until the lamb is tender.

Stir in the olives, lemon zest and juice, and chopped parsley 1 minute before the end of cooking.

Meanwhile, bring the measured water to a boil in another saucepan and pour in the grits. Cook, stirring continuously, for 1 minute. Stir in the butter and grated Parmesan and divide among 4 bowls.

Spoon the lamb stew over the grits and serve.

For lamb cutlets with Italian-style fried polenta,

heat 2 tablespoons olive oil in a skillet and cook 8 slices of prepared polenta for 2 minutes on each side. Remove and keep warm. Add 1 tablespoon olive oil to the same pan and cook 1 finely diced onion and 1 finely diced red chile for 1 minute before adding 8 lamb cutlets (3–4 oz each) and a sprinkling of dried oregano. Cook the lamb for 2 minutes on each side. Sprinkle in a dash of red wine and 2 tablespoons chopped pitted black ripe olives. Serve the cutlets with the fried polenta.
Total cooking time 15 minutes.

ham with apricot relish & potatoes

Serves **4**

Total cooking time **25 minutes**

4 **all-purpose potatoes**
(about 1 lb), peeled and cut
into cubes

1 lb **cured ham**, cut into
4 steaks

3 tablespoons **vegetable oil**

1 **onion**, coarsely chopped

1 (15 oz) can **apricots in
juice**, drained and juice
reserved

1 teaspoon **ground cinnamon**

2 teaspoons **paprika**

3 tablespoons chopped **flat
leaf parsley**

salt and **black pepper**

Bring a large saucepan of lightly salted water to a boil and cook the potatoes for 10 minutes. Drain.

Meanwhile, cook the ham under a preheated hot broiler for 5–6 minutes on each side until cooked and heated through.

While the potatoes and ham are cooking, heat 1 tablespoon of the oil in a large, heavy saucepan and cook the onion over medium heat, stirring frequently, for 3–4 minutes, until softened. Add the apricot juice and cinnamon and cook over high heat for 3 minutes to reduce the liquid by half. Remove from the heat and add the apricots, then pour all the mixture into a food processor or blender and process to a thick, textured sauce. Return to the saucepan and heat through gently while finishing the potatoes.

Heat the remaining oil in a large, heavy skillet and cook the drained potatoes over high heat, stirring frequently, for 5 minutes, until golden and crisp. Sprinkle with the paprika, season with black pepper, and toss in the flat leaf parsley.

Spoon the sauce over the ham to serve, accompanied by the paprika potatoes.

For apricot-glazed ham, warm 2 tablespoons apricot preserves in a small saucepan, then stir in ½ teaspoon ground cumin and season with black pepper. Cook 4 cured ham steaks (about 4 oz each), under a preheated hot broiler, brushing frequently with the glaze, for 5–6 minutes on each side, until cooked and heated through. Serve with prepared couscous. **Total cooking time 10 minutes.**

pan-fried gnocchi & chorizo salad

Serves **4**

Total cooking time **15 minutes**

2 tablespoons **olive oil**
1 (16 oz) package **gnocchi**
4 large, **ripe tomatoes**,
   coarsely chopped
1 small bunch of **basil leaves**,
   coarsely shredded
4 oz **mozzarella cheese**, torn
   into pieces
4 oz sliced **chorizo sausage**
1–2 tablespoons **balsamic
   vinegar**
salt and **black pepper**

Heat the olive oil in a large, nonstick skillet and add the gnocchi. Pan-fry for about 8 minutes, moving frequently, until crisp and golden.

Meanwhile, toss the tomatoes with the shredded basil and torn mozzarella, season, and arrange on 4 serving plates.

Add the chorizo to the pan of gnocchi for the final 1–2 minutes of cooking, until slightly crisp and golden.

Sprinkle the gnocchi and chorizo over the salads, then serve drizzled with the balsamic vinegar.

For baked creamy gnocchi & chorizo, dice 4 large tomatoes and put into a large bowl with 4 oz sliced chorizo sausage, 1 ½ (1 lb) packages gnocchi, 1 small bunch of basil leaves, coarsely shredded, and 1–2 tablespoons balsamic vinegar. Season generously, then transfer to a large ovenproof dish, pour ⅔ cup light cream over the gnocchi, and sprinkle with 4 oz mozzarella cheese, torn into pieces. Cook in a preheated oven, at 400°F, for about 20 minutes, until bubbling and golden. Serve with plenty of mixed salad greens. **Total cooking time 30 minutes.**

rack of lamb with harissa

Serves **4**

Total cooking time **30 minutes**

1 cup **hazelnuts**

½ cup **sesame seeds**

2 tablespoons **coriander seeds**

1 tablespoon **cumin seeds**

¼ cup **olive oil**

2 **racks of lamb**
(7–8 ribs each)

2 **red bell peppers**, cored, seeded, and thickly sliced

2 tablespoons **harissa paste**

⅓ cup **plain yogurt**

salt and **black pepper**

couscous, to serve (optional)

Put the nuts and spices in a small, dry skillet and toast for 1 minute. Transfer to a mortar and crush coarsely with a pestle, adding a little salt.

Rub 2 tablespoons of the oil over the lamb racks, season well, and press the nut mixture onto the fatty side of each rack. Transfer to a shallow roasting pan and roast in a preheated oven, at 425°F, for 10 minutes. Arrange the bell peppers around the lamb and return to the oven for an additional 10–15 minutes for rare to medium lamb.

Swirl the harissa over the yogurt in a bowl. Slice the lamb racks and serve with the bell peppers, drizzling with the harissa sauce. Serve with couscous, if desired.

For easy spiced lamb pilaf, heat 1 tablespoon olive oil in a flameproof casserole, add 1 tablespoon harissa paste, then add 12 oz boneless leg of lamb pieces. Stir around the pan until well coated, then stir in 1½ cups basmati rice or other long-grain rice. Pour in 2½ cups chicken broth and bring to a boil. Let simmer, uncovered, for 10 minutes. Stir in 1 (5 oz) package baby spinach, reduce the heat to low, cover, and cook for an additional 5 minutes, until the rice is tender. Sprinkle with mint and drizzle with plain yogurt to serve. **Total cooking time 20 minutes.**

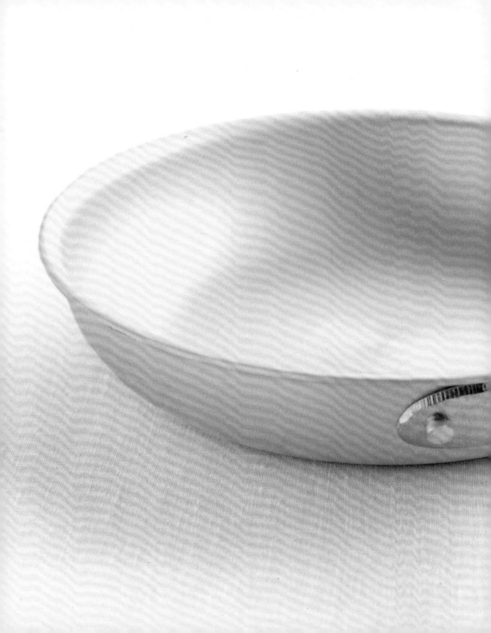

fish & seafood

stuffed mussels

Serves **4**
Total cooking time **30 minutes**

2–3 lb large **fresh mussels**
   (about 48 mussels),
   scrubbed and debearded
1 ½ cups **fresh white bread
   crumbs**
½ cup **walnut pieces**
1 ¾ sticks (7 oz) **butter**
6 **garlic cloves**, chopped
juice of 1 **lemon**
2 tablespoons grated
   Parmesan cheese
2 tablespoons chopped
   tarragon
small handful of **parsley**,
   chopped

Place the mussels into a large saucepan, discarding any that are cracked or don't shut when tapped, cover, and steam for 5 minutes, shaking the pan occasionally, until they have opened, then drain. Discard any that remain closed. Break off the empty half of the shells and place the mussels on a large baking sheet.

Put the bread crumbs, walnuts, butter, garlic, lemon juice, and grated Parmesan into a food processor and process until the mixture starts to come together. Add the herbs and blend until combined.

Divide the herb mixture among the mussels, making sure each mussel is covered. Cook under a preheated hot broiler for 2–3 minutes, until the stuffing is golden brown. You may need to cook the mussels in batches if you cannot fit them all on the baking sheet at once.

Serve immediately.

For smoked mussel bruschetta, toast 8 slices of ciabatta on both sides, then rub each slice with a garlic clove. Coarsely chop 8 oz smoked mussels and mix with 2 coarsely chopped tomatoes, 1 tablespoon chopped parsley, and the juice of ½ lemon. Spoon the mussel mixture onto the toast and serve topped with a few arugula leaves. **Total cooking time 10 minutes.**

halibut ceviche with grapefruit

Serves **2**

Total cooking time **25 minutes**

1 lb **skinless halibut fillet**
2 **limes**
1 **grapefruit**
6 **cherry tomatoes**, halved
1 **red chile,** seeded (optional)
  and sliced
handful of **mint**, finely sliced
1 tablespoon **extra virgin**
  olive oil
salt and **black pepper**

Using a sharp knife, cut the fish into thin slices.

Grate the zest from 1 lime into a nonmetallic bowl, then squeeze in the juice from both limes. Cut off the bottom of the grapefruit, then cut around the flesh to remove the zest and pith. Slice into segments and set aside. Add any juice from the grapefruit to the bowl.

Add the fish to the lime and grapefruit juices and toss to coat. Cover and let marinate in the refrigerator for 15 minutes.

Discard the marinade from the fish. Arrange the fish on a serving plate with the grapefruit segments and tomatoes. Sprinkle with the chile and mint, season, and drizzle with the oil to serve.

For spicy halibut & grapefruit salad, mix together 1 tablespoon vegetable oil, ½ finely chopped red chile, and a handful of fresh cilantro, finely chopped. Toss with 1 lb skinless halibut fillet, cut into bite-size pieces. Cook under a preheated hot broiler for 2–3 minutes on each side. Meanwhile, peel 3 segments of grapefruit and cut into small pieces. Whisk together 1 tablespoon vegetable oil and 1 tablespoon rice vinegar. Toss with 3½ cups mixed salad greens and another handful of cilantro, top with the grapefruit and halibut, and serve. **Total cooking time 15 minutes.**

shrimp & avocado tostada

Serves **4**

Total cooking time **10 minutes**

4 large **soft flour tortillas**

1 small **iceberg lettuce**, shredded

10 oz **cooked, peeled shrimp**

1 large, **ripe but firm avocado**, pitted, peeled, and diced

2 tablespoons chopped **fresh cilantro**

1 tablespoon **lime juice**

salt and **cracked black pepper**

lime wedges, to serve

Heat a ridged grill pan and then toast a tortilla for 30–60 seconds on each side until lightly charred. Immediately push it into a small, deep bowl and set aside. Repeat with the remaining tortillas to make 4 bowl-shape tortillas. Place one-quarter of the shredded lettuce inside each one.

Meanwhile, toss together the shrimp, avocado, cilantro, and lime juice, and season.

Divide the shrimp and avocado mixture among the tortillas and serve with lime wedges for squeezing over the tostada.

For shrimp & black bean chili, heat 2 tablespoons vegetable oil in a large skillet and add 4 chopped scallions, 2 chopped garlic cloves, and 1 finely seeded and chopped red chile. Cook gently for 2 minutes, until softened, then add 1 (14½ oz) can diced tomatoes and 1 (15 oz) can black beans, rinsed and drained. Simmer gently for 10–12 minutes, until thickened slightly. Stir in 3 tablespoons chopped fresh cilantro, 1 tablespoon lime juice, and 8 oz cooked, peeled shrimp. Simmer for 1 minute, until the shrimp are hot, and serve with grilled tortillas and lime wedges, sprinkled with extra cilantro. **Total cooking time 25 minutes.**

manhattan clam chowder

Serves **4**

Total cooking time **30 minutes**

1 tablespoon **vegetable oil**

4 oz **bacon**, chopped

1 large **onion**, chopped

1 **celery stick**, chopped

1 **carrot**, peeled and chopped

3 **Yukon Gold** or **white round potatoes**, peeled and chopped

1 (14½ oz) can **diced tomatoes**

1 **thyme sprig**

6½ cups **fish broth**

1 lb **fresh clams**, scrubbed

½ cup **dry white wine**

salt and **black pepper**

crusty bread or **crackers**, to serve (optional)

Heat the oil in a large saucepan, add the bacon, and cook for 2 minutes, until browned. Stir in the onion, celery, and carrot and cook for an additional 5 minutes until softened.

Add the potatoes, tomatoes, thyme, and broth. Cook for 12–15 minutes, until the potatoes are soft.

Meanwhile, put the clams into a large saucepan, discarding any that are cracked or don't shut when tapped. Add the wine, cover, and cook for 5 minutes or until the clams have opened. Discard any that remain closed. Remove the clam meat from most of the shells, keeping some in their shells for decoration, and reserve the juice.

Season the chowder and add the clam meat, whole clams, and clam juice to the pan. Heat through and serve with crusty bread or crackers, if desired.

For clam & tomato linguine, heat 1 tablespoon olive oil in a large saucepan, add 2 crushed garlic cloves, and cook for 30 seconds. Add ½ cup dry white wine and 1 lb scrubbed fresh clams, discarding any that are cracked or don't shut when tapped. Cover and cook for 5 minutes, shaking the pan occasionally, or until the clams have opened. Discard any that remain closed. Stir in 1 tablespoon lemon juice and 10 cherry tomatoes, halved. Cook 1 lb fresh linguine according to the package directions until al dente, then drain, reserving a little cooking water. Stir into the clams with 2 tablespoons butter and the reserved pasta cooking water, if needed. Sprinkle with some chopped parsley and serve. **Total cooking time 15 minutes.**

sesame tuna with ginger dressing

Serves **6**

Total cooking time **25 minutes**

1¾ lb piece of **fresh tuna**

2 tablespoons **vegetable oil**

3 tablespoons **white sesame seeds**

3 tablespoons **black sesame seeds**

½ **cucumber**, sliced into ribbons

2 **avocados**, pitted, peeled, and sliced

2 **scallions**, shredded

salt and **black pepper**

For the dressing

1 **garlic clove**, crushed

1 **chile,** seeded and finely chopped

1 teaspoon finely chopped **fresh ginger root**

1 tablespoon **soy sauce**

juice of ½ **lime**

1 teaspoon grated **orange zest**

1 tablespoon **honey**

1 tablespoon **sesame oil**

Season the tuna. Heat the oil in a large skillet, add the tuna, and cook for 3–5 minutes or until browned all over.

Spread the sesame seeds on a plate and press the seared tuna into them until well coated. Put on a baking sheet and cook in a preheated oven, at 425°F, for 10–12 minutes, until browned but still pink inside.

Mix together the ingredients for the dressing. Cut the tuna into thick slices and arrange on serving plates with the cucumber and avocado slices and scallions. Drizzle with the dressing to serve.

For tuna carpaccio with ginger salad, cut 1¼ lb fresh tuna into ½ inch steaks, put between 2 pieces of plastic wrap, and pound gently until thin. Arrange on serving plates. Whisk together the juice of 1 orange and 1 lime and 1 teaspoon each finely chopped fresh ginger root, rice vinegar, and soy sauce. Toss with 7 cups arugula and 1 (6 oz) package radishes, sliced. Arrange on top of the tuna and sprinkle with toasted sesame seeds. **Total cooking time 10 minutes.**

spicy spaghetti vongole

Serves **4**
Total cooking time **20 minutes**

1 lb **dried spaghetti**
⅓ cup **extra virgin olive oil**, plus extra to serve
2 **garlic cloves**, chopped
2 **red chiles**, seeded and finely chopped
4 **anchovy fillets in oil**, drained and chopped
small handful of **flat leaf parsley**, finely chopped
2 lb **fresh clams**, scrubbed
½ cup **dry white wine**
salt and **black pepper**

Cook the pasta according to the package directions until firm but still tender. Drain, then return to the pan.

Meanwhile, heat the oil in a skillet, add the garlic, red chiles, anchovies, and half the parsley, and cook gently for a couple of minutes. Add the clams to the pan, discarding any that are cracked or don't shut when tapped. Pour in the wine, cover, and cook over medium heat for 5 minutes, shaking the pan occasionally, or until the clams have opened. Discard any that remain closed.

Add the clams and the juices to the spaghetti with the remaining parsley, then season and toss to mix well. Divide into warm bowls, drizzle with a little extra oil, and serve immediately.

For spicy garlic-braised clams, heat 2 tablespoons olive oil in a heavy saucepan, add 4 chopped shallots, and cook over medium heat, stirring occasionally, for 6–8 minutes, until softened. Add 2 crushed garlic cloves and 2 seeded and finely chopped red chiles and cook, stirring, for 1–2 minutes. Stir in 2 tablespoons tomato paste and 4 finely chopped plum tomatoes and cook for an additional 8–10 minutes. Add 2 cups hot fish broth and 1¾ lb scrubbed fresh clams, discarding any that are cracked or don't shut when tapped, then bring to a boil, cover and cook over medium heat for 5 minutes or until the clams have opened. Discard any that remain closed. Season, ladle into warm bowls, and serve. **Total cooking time 30 minutes.**

salt-baked bream

SUBSTITUTE A DIFFERENT KIND OF FISH

Serves **4**
Total cooking time **30 minutes**

9 cups (4 lb) **kosher salt**
1 tablespoon **fennel seeds**
2 **egg whites**, lightly beaten
2 **sea bream**, gutted and
   scaled
1 **lemon**
1 **lime**
1 **orange**
½ **fennel bulb**, trimmed and
   thinly sliced
¼ cup **extra virgin olive oil**
handful of **chives**, chopped
salt and **black pepper**

Mix together the kosher salt and fennel seeds in a bowl, then stir through the egg whites. Spread about one-third of this mixture over a baking sheet or the bottom of a large ovenproof dish. Place the fish on top, then cover with the remaining salt mixture, making sure you don't have any gaps, although it's fine for the tails to be showing. Bake in a preheated oven, at 400°F, for 20 minutes.

Meanwhile, cut the peel from the citrus fruits, using a sharp knife. Divide the fruits into segments by cutting between the membranes, holding them over a bowl to catch the juice. Put into the bowl with the juice, add the remaining ingredients, and season.

Crack open the salt crust by giving it a sharp tap with the back of a heavy knife. Peel away the salt crust, remove the fish, and serve with the dressed citrus segments and fennel alongside.

For sea bream baked on salt, spread 4½ cups (2 lb) kosher salt over a baking sheet. Trim and thinly slice 1 fennel bulb and put it on top of the salt with some thyme sprigs. Lay 4 sea bream fillets on top, skin side up, and bake in a preheated oven, at 400°F, for 10–12 minutes, until the fish just starts to flake. Carefully lift the fish off the salt, squeeze a little lemon juice over the fish, and serve. **Total cooking time 20 minutes.**

mackerel with roasted tomatoes

Serves **4**

Total cooking time **30 minutes**

12 **plum tomatoes**, halved

3 tablespoons **olive oil**, plus
   extra for oiling

1 teaspoon **sugar**

1 teaspoon **red wine vinegar**

4 **mackerel fillets** (about
   5 oz each)

⅔ cup **crème fraîche** or
   Greek yogurt

1–2 tablespoons **horseradish
   sauce**

3 cups **arugula**

salt and **black pepper**

Put the tomatoes onto a lightly oiled baking sheet. Drizzle with 2 tablespoons of the oil, then sprinkle each tomato half with the sugar and vinegar. Place in a preheated oven, at 400°F, for 20–25 minutes, until browned and soft.

Meanwhile, heat a large, dry skillet until hot. Rub the remaining oil over the mackerel and season well. Add the mackerel to the pan, skin side down, and cook for 5 minutes, until the skin is golden brown. Turn over and cook for an additional 3 minutes or until the fish is cooked through.

Stir together the crème fraîche or yogurt and horseradish sauce.

Arrange the arugula, roasted tomatoes, and mackerel on serving plates and serve with spoonfuls of the horseradish sauce on the side.

For mackerel & sun-dried tomato salad, gently toss together 1 (4½ oz) can drained mackerel in olive oil, ½ cup drained, chopped sun-dried tomatoes in oil, and 4 cups arugula. Whisk together the juice of ½ lemon, 3 tablespoons olive oil, and 1 tablespoon horseradish sauce. Drizzle the dressing over the salad to serve. **Total cooking time 10 minutes.**

honey mustard salmon

Serves **4**
Total cooking time **10 minutes**

4 **salmon fillets** (about
  5 oz each)
olive oil, for oiling
2 tablespoons **whole-grain
  mustard**
2 tablespoons **honey**
handful of **dill**, chopped
salt and **black pepper**

To serve (optional)
new potatoes
cucumber salad

Put the salmon into a lightly oiled baking pan and season. Mix together the mustard, honey, and dill and drizzle the sauce over the salmon. Roast in a preheated oven, at 425°F, for 8 minutes or until cooked through.

Serve with some new potatoes and a cucumber salad, if desired.

For salmon with mustard Hollandaise, put 4 thin salmon fillets (about 4 oz each), onto a lightly oiled baking sheet, drizzle with 2 tablespoons olive oil, and season. Place in a preheated oven, at 250°F, for 25–30 minutes, until just cooked through. Meanwhile, for the sauce, crack 2 egg yolks into a heatproof bowl set snugly over a saucepan of simmering water. Add a squeeze of lemon juice and then slowly whisk in 1 stick (4 oz) melted butter until the sauce has thickened. Stir in 1 teaspoon whole-grain mustard and more lemon juice to taste. Serve with the salmon. **Total cooking time 30 minutes.**

clams in black bean sauce

Serves **4**

Total cooking time **10 minutes**

2 tablespoons **vegetable oil**

2 **scallions**

2 **garlic cloves**, crushed

2 teaspoons finely chopped
fresh ginger root

1 **red chile,** finely chopped

1 tablespoon **prepared
black bean sauce**

2 lb **fresh clams,** scrubbed

3 tablespoons **chicken broth**

1 tablespoon **soy sauce**

1 tablespoon **Chinese
rice wine**

fresh cilantro leaves,
to garnish

Heat the oil in a large saucepan over high heat.
Meanwhile, slice the scallions and separate the white
and green parts. Add the white scallion, garlic, ginger,
and chile to the pan and cook briefly until sizzling. Stir
in the black bean sauce, then add the clams, discarding
any that are cracked or don't shut when tapped, along
with the remaining ingredients.

Cover the pan and cook over medium heat for
5 minutes, shaking the pan occasionally, or until the
clams have opened. Discard any that remain closed.

Divide the clams onto serving plates and sprinkle with
the green scallion and cilantro to serve.

For mussels in black bean sauce, rinse 1 tablespoon
fermented black beans. Mash with a little sugar. Briefly
cook 2 sliced scallions, 2 crushed garlic cloves, and
2 teaspoons each finely chopped fresh root ginger
and red chile in 2 tablespoons hot vegetable oil in
a saucepan. Add the beans, 3 tablespoons chicken
broth, and 2 tablespoons each soy sauce and Chinese
rice wine. Bring to a boil, then simmer for 5 minutes.
Meanwhile, heat 2 tablespoons vegetable oil in a
large saucepan. Add 2 lb scrubbed fresh mussels,
discarding any that are cracked or don't shut when
tapped, along with 3 tablespoons hot water. Cover
and cook over medium heat for 5 minutes, shaking
the pan occasionally, or until opened. Discard any that
remain closed and the top shells. Drizzle with the sauce.
Total cooking time 20 minutes.

creamy scallops with leeks

Serves **4**
Total cooking time **15 minutes**

4 tablespoons **butter**
16 **shelled and cleaned scallops**, halved
1 **rindless bacon slice**, coarsely snipped
3 **leeks**, trimmed, cleaned, and sliced
1 cup **crème fraîche** or **heavy cream**
finely grated zest of **1 lemon**
black pepper
instant long-grain rice, to serve

Melt half the butter in a large, heavy skillet and cook the scallops and bacon over high heat, stirring frequently, for about 2 minutes, until just golden brown and cooked through. Remove with a slotted spoon and keep warm.

Add the remaining butter to the pan and cook the leeks over medium heat, stirring occasionally, for 5 minutes, until softened and lightly browned in places. Add the crème fraîche or heavy cream and lemon zest and season generously with black pepper.

Return the scallops to the pan and toss into the creamy leeks. Serve immediately with cooked rice.

For scallop & bacon kebabs with leeks, cut 10 smoked bacon slices in half and wrap each around 20 shelled and cleaned small scallops. Thread onto 4 metal skewers. Mix 2 tablespoons olive oil with 1 tablespoon honey and brush over the bacon. Melt 2 tablespoons butter with 1 tablespoon olive oil in a skillet and cook 2 trimmed, cleaned, and finely sliced leeks, stirring, for 6–8 minutes, until soft and golden brown. Add 1 teaspoon each finely grated lemon zest and whole-grain mustard and 1 cup crème fraîche or heavy cream and heat for 2 minutes. Keep warm. Heat a ridged grill pan over high heat and cook the skewers for 2–3 minutes on each side, until brown and cooked through. Serve on a bed of the creamy leeks. **Total cooking time 30 minutes.**

swordfish with salsa verde

Serves **4**

Total cooking time **20 minutes**

1½ teaspoons **Dijon mustard**
2 cups **extra virgin olive oil**
~~4 anchovy fillets in oil,~~
   ~~drained and chopped~~
handful each of **parsley, basil,**
   mint, and **tarragon**
2 tablespoons drained **capers**
1 **garlic clove**, crushed
2 tablespoons **olive oil**
4 **swordfish steaks** (about
   5 oz each)
juice of 1 **lemon**
salt and **black pepper**
crisp green salad, to serve

N O

Whisk together the mustard and 1 cup of the extra virgin olive oil in a bowl until they have emulsified. ~~Stir in the anchovies.~~

Chop the herbs and capers together and then add them to the oil mixture along with the crushed garlic. Gradually add more of the extra virgin olive oil until the sauce has a spooning consistency.

Heat a ridged grill pan until hot. Brush the swordfish steaks on both sides with the olive oil and season well. Grill the steaks for ~~2–3 minutes~~ on each side or until cooked through but still moist. *6–7 minutes*

Add the lemon juice to the salsa verde and serve spooned over the grilled fish with a crisp green salad.

For swordfish with quick salsa verde, cook 4 swordfish steaks (about 5 oz each), under a preheated hot broiler for 2–3 minutes on each side, until cooked through. Meanwhile, put 2 peeled garlic cloves, a small handful of drained capers, a small handful of drained pickles, 4 drained anchovy fillets in oil, 2 large handfuls of parsley, a handful each of basil and mint, 1 tablespoon Dijon mustard, 3 tablespoons white wine vinegar, ½ cup extra virgin olive oil, and some salt and black pepper into a food processor or blender. Process until fully mixed and serve with the swordfish. **Total cooking time 10 minutes.**

creamy spiced lobster tail

Serves **4**
Total cooking time **20 minutes**

2 **egg yolks**, beaten
½ cup **heavy cream**
2 tablespoons **butter**
2 tablespoons **dry sherry**
½ teaspoon **salt**
1 tablespoon **medium curry powder**
¼ cup finely chopped **fresh cilantro**, plus extra to garnish
1 lb **cooked lobster tail meat**, cut into bite-size pieces

To serve
lemon wedges
steamed **rice**

Whisk together the egg yolks and heavy cream in a small bowl until well blended. Melt the butter in a saucepan over low heat, then stir in the egg mixture and sherry. Cook, stirring, for 10–12 minutes or until the mixture thickens, but do not let it boil.

Remove from the heat, then stir in the salt, curry powder, and cilantro. Stir in the lobster, then return the pan to low heat and cook gently until heated through.

Spoon into warm bowls, sprinkle with chopped cilantro, and serve with lemon wedges to squeeze over the lobster and steamed rice.

For spicy lobster gratin, melt 4 tablespoons butter in a saucepan over low heat, add 2 tablespoons all-purpose flour and 2 tablespoons medium or hot curry powder, and cook, stirring, for 1–2 minutes. Gradually whisk in 1 cup heavy cream and ½ cup milk and cook, stirring continuously, for about 5 minutes or until thickened. Cut 1 lb cooked lobster tail meat into large pieces and add to the pan. Toss to mix well, season, and pour into a shallow casserole dish. Sprinkle with 4 cups fresh white bread crumbs and place in a preheated oven, at 425°F, for 15–20 minutes or until bubbling. Serve warm with a crisp green salad. **Total cooking time 30 minutes.**

red snapper with dill sauce

Serves **4**

Total cooking time **10 minutes**

4 **red snapper fillets** (about
5 oz each)
2 tablespoons **olive oil**
⅓ cup **plain yogurt**
juice of ½ **lemon**
2 **garlic cloves**, crushed
handful of **dill**, finely chopped
salt and **black pepper**
grilled **zucchini**, to serve

Season the fish fillets, then rub them all over with
1 tablespoon of the oil. Cook, skin side down, in a ridged
grill pan over high heat for 5 minutes. Turn over and cook
for an additional 5 minutes, until just cooked through.

Meanwhile, mix together the remaining oil, yogurt, lemon
juice, garlic, and dill, then season.

Spoon the dill sauce over the fish fillets and serve with
grilled zucchini.

For Indian yogurt-baked cod, mix together 1¼ cups
plain yogurt, 2 tablespoons ground coriander, 2 teaspoons
ground cumin, 1 finely chopped green chile, and 1 teaspoon
finely chopped fresh ginger root. Place 4 thick haddock
fillets (about 6 oz each) in an oiled baking dish. Season and
pour the yogurt mixture over the fish. Cut 3 tablespoons
butter into small pieces and dot over the fish fillets. Cover
the dish with aluminum foil and place in a preheated oven,
at 375°F, for 20 minutes, until just cooked through. Transfer
the fish to a serving plate. Stir a little more melted butter into
the yogurt if it has split, then sprinkle with chopped fresh
cilantro and serve. **Total cooking time 30 minutes.**

peppered tuna

Serves **4**

Total cooking time ~~28~~ **20 minutes**

⅓ cup **extra virgin olive oil**

12 oz **fresh tuna steak**

1 tablespoon **black peppercorns**, coarsely crushed

1 tablespoon **balsamic vinegar**

3½ cups **arugula**

salt

Parmesan cheese shavings, to serve

Brush 1 tablespoon of the oil over the tuna. Place the crushed peppercorns on a plate, then roll the tuna in the peppercorns until well coated. Wrap up tightly in a piece of aluminum foil. Heat a dry, heavy skillet until smoking hot. Add the wrapped tuna to the pan and cook for 2 minutes, turning every minute or so to cook evenly on each side. Remove from the pan and let cool a little.

Whisk the remaining oil with the vinegar until well combined, then season with salt. Just before serving, unwrap the tuna and slice. Toss the arugula with the dressing and arrange on serving plates. Top the greens with the tuna and sprinkle with Parmesan shavings to serve.

For slow-cooked tuna with arugula pesto, rub 1 tablespoon olive oil over 4 thick, fresh tuna steaks (about 6 oz each), put onto a baking sheet, and season well. Place in a preheated oven, at 225°F, for 25 minutes. Meanwhile, in a food processor or blender, process together 3½ cups arugula, 2 tablespoons grated Parmesan cheese, and a good squeeze of lemon juice. Stir in ⅓ cup olive oil and 1 teaspoon drained capers and spoon the pesto over the tuna to serve. **Total cooking time 30 minutes.**

flounder florentine

Serves **4**

Total cooking time **25 minutes**

1 tablespoon **butter**, plus
   extra for greasing
1 tablespoon **all-purpose**
   flour
⅔ cup **milk**
½ cup shredded **cheddar**
   cheese
½ (10 oz) package **frozen**
   spinach
2 large **flounder fillets**
   (about 6 oz each), halved
   to make 4 thin fillets
¼ cup grated **Parmesan**
   cheese
salt and **black pepper**
mashed **potatoes**, to serve

Melt the butter in a saucepan. Stir in the flour and cook for 2 minutes. Slowly whisk in the milk until smooth. Bring to a boil, whisking, then simmer for a few minutes, until thickened. Take off the heat, stir in the cheddar, and season.

Put the spinach into a strainer and pour boiling water over it until defrosted. Drain well, then coarsely chop. Put the fish onto a lightly greased baking sheet. Spread a layer of spinach on top of each fillet, then drizzle with some of the cheese sauce. Sprinkle with the Parmesan.

Bake in a preheated oven, at 400°F, for 10–12 minutes, until the fish is just cooked through. Serve immediately with mashed potatoes.

For flounder with simple parsley sauce, smear a little butter over 4 flounder fillets (about 6 oz each). Cook under a preheated hot broiler for 7–10 minutes, until just cooked through. Meanwhile, mix ¼ cup crème fraîche or Greek yogurt with a large handful of parsley, chopped, and a little milk to loosen. Spoon the sauce over the fish and serve alongside some lightly cooked spinach and drained and mashed canned lima beans warmed through in a saucepan. **Total cooking time 10 minutes.**

monkfish with lentils

Serves **4**

Total cooking time **30 minutes**

4 skinless **monkfish fillets**
  (about 5 oz each)
juice of 1 **lemon**
6–8 **basil leaves**, chopped,
  plus extra, torn, to garnish
2 teaspoons **freshly ground
  black pepper**
4 slices of **prosciutto**, halved
  lengthwise
¼ cup **olive oil**
2 **shallots**, diced
2 cups **cooked green lentils**
7 cups **baby spinach**
2 tablespoons **crème fraîche
  or Greek yogurt**
salt

Sprinkle the monkfish with half the lemon juice, the basil, and black pepper. Wrap each fillet in 2 slices of prosciutto and chill for 10 minutes.

Meanwhile, heat half the olive oil in a skillet and sauté the shallots for 3–4 minutes. Stir in the lentils and cook for 2–3 minutes to heat through.

Stir the spinach into the lentils, letting it wilt. Squeeze the remaining lemon juice over the lentils, stir in the crème fraîche or yogurt, and season with salt.

Heat the remaining olive oil in another skillet and cook the wrapped monkfish for 6–8 minutes, turning over 2–3 times, until cooked through.

Serve the wrapped monkfish on a bed of lentils and spinach, sprinkled with torn basil leaves.

For monkfish fillets in a smoky tomato sauce, heat 2 tablespoons olive oil in a skillet and sauté 2 finely diced shallots for 3–4 minutes. Add 2 crushed garlic cloves, ½ teaspoon smoked paprika, and 1 cored, seeded, and thinly sliced red bell pepper. Pour in 1 (14½ oz) can diced tomatoes and simmer for 5–6 minutes. Stir in 2 cups shredded spinach leaves and cook until wilted. Meanwhile, heat 1 tablespoon olive oil in another skillet and cook 1 lb monkfish fillet, cut into 1 inch chunks, for 1–2 minutes on each side. Transfer the monkfish to the tomato sauce and stir in gently. Stir in 2 tablespoons chopped parsley and serve on a bed of cooked green lentils. **Total cooking time 20 minutes.**

grilled sea bass with salsa verde

Serves **4**
Total cooking time **20 minutes**

olive oil, for oiling
4 sea bass fillets (about
    5 oz each)
salt and **black pepper**

For the salsa verde
3 tablespoons **olive oil**
large handful of **flat leaf
    parsley**
small handful of **basil**
1 **garlic clove**, crushed
juice of ½ **lemon**
1 tablespoon drained **capers**

To serve
boiled **new potatoes**
green salad

Rub a little olive oil over the fish fillets and season.
Heat a ridged grill pan until smoking hot. Grill the fish
fillets, skin side down, for 7 minutes, until the skin is
crisp and golden brown. Turn over and cook for an
additional 5 minutes, until just cooked through.

Meanwhile, process together the salsa verde
ingredients in a small food processor or blender until
you have a coarse paste.

Place the fish on serving plates and spoon the salsa
verde over them. Serve with boiled new potatoes and
a green salad.

For sea bass stuffed with salsa verde, prepare the
salsa verde as above. Divide 2 sea bass (about 2½ lb
each), gutted and scaled, into fillets and season. Thinly
slice 1 lemon and lay half the slices down a lightly
oiled baking sheet. Cover with 2 fish fillets, skin side
down. Spread the salsa verde all over the fish, then
lay the other fillets on top, skin side up. Cover with the
remaining lemon slices. Cook in a preheated oven, at
450°F, for 15–20 minutes, until just cooked through.
Place on a warm serving platter and serve with boiled
new potatoes and a green salad. **Total cooking time
30 minutes.**

crab claws in spicy tomato sauce

Serves **4**

Total cooking time **25 minutes**

2 tablespoons **vegetable oil**
1¼ lb **raw crab claws**
3 **garlic cloves**, crushed
1 tablespoon finely chopped
  fresh ginger root
2–3 **red chiles**, seeded
  (optional) and finely chopped
¾ cup canned **diced**
  tomatoes
1 tablespoon **soy sauce**
1 tablespoon **Chinese**
  rice wine
1 tablespoon packed
  dark brown sugar
2 teaspoons **rice vinegar** or
  apple cider vinegar
2 teaspoons **cornstarch**
1 tablespoon **water**
2 **scallions**, shredded
plain rice, to serve

Heat the oil in a large wok or skillet. Add the crab claws and cook for about 2 minutes, until bright red. Remove from the pan and set aside. Add the garlic and ginger and stir-fry for 30 seconds, then add the chiles followed by the tomatoes, soy sauce, Chinese rice wine, sugar, and vinegar. Simmer for 10 minutes, adding a little water, if necessary.

Return the crab to the pan and cook for an additional 8 minutes, until cooked through.

Mix together the cornstarch and measured water until smooth. Stir into the pan and cook for 1 minute, until the sauce is slightly thickened. Sprinkle with the scallions and serve with plain rice.

For sweet & sour spicy crab claws, heat
2 tablespoons vegetable oil in a large wok or skillet. Stir-fry 3 crushed garlic cloves and 1 tablespoon finely chopped fresh ginger root for 30 seconds. Add 1 lb cooked crab claws, 2 tablespoons each ketchup, sweet chili sauce, and water and a pinch of sugar. Heat through. Squeeze lime juice over the crab to taste and sprinkle with chopped fresh cilantro. **Total cooking time 10 minutes.**

lobster thermidor

Serves **4**

Total cooking time **20 minutes**

1 tablespoon **butter**
1 tablespoon **olive oil**
1 **shallot**, finely chopped
3 tablespoons **dry sherry**
1 teaspoon **Dijon mustard**
½ cup **crème fraîche**
  or **heavy cream**
2 small **cooked lobsters**
  (about 1¼ lb each)
½ cup shredded **Gruyère**
  cheese
salt

Heat the butter and oil in a small saucepan. Add the shallot and cook for 5 minutes, until softened. Pour in the sherry and cook for 2 minutes, until nearly boiled away. Stir in the mustard and crème fraîche or heavy cream, heat through, and season with salt.

Meanwhile, using a large knife, cut the lobsters lengthwise in half. Remove the meat from the tail and claws, reserving the main shell halves. Cut the lobster meat into large chunks.

Add the lobster meat to the sauce and warm through. Carefully spoon into the tail cavities of the reserved lobster shell halves and sprinkle with the Gruyère. Cook under a preheated hot broiler for 3–5 minutes, until golden and bubbling.   5~8

For lobster with thermidor butter, mix together 2 tablespoons softened butter and ¼ cup grated Parmesan cheese, 1 tablespoon crème fraîche or heavy cream, 1 teaspoon Dijon mustard, a squeeze of lemon juice, and a pinch of paprika. Use a large knife to cut 2 cooked lobsters (about 1¼ lb each), lengthwise in half. Remove the meat from the claws and tuck around the tail meat. Dot the thermidor butter all over. Cook under a preheated hot broiler for 3–5 minutes, until golden and bubbling, then serve. **Total cooking time 15 minutes.**

hot-smoked salmon kedgeree

Serves **4**

Total cooking time **30 minutes**

3 tablespoons boiling **water**
pinch of **saffron threads**
1 tablespoon **vegetable oil**
2 tablespoons **butter**
1 **onion**, finely chopped
1 **garlic clove**, finely chopped
1 teaspoon finely grated **fresh ginger root**
1 teaspoon **mild curry powder**
1⅓ cups **basmati rice** or **other long-grain rice**
3 cups **fish or vegetable broth**
6 **quail eggs**
10 oz **hot-smoked salmon fillets**, skinned
⅓ cup **crème fraîche** or **Greek yogurt**
salt and **black pepper**
chopped **flat leaf parsley**, to garnish

Pour the measured water over the saffron in a small bowl and let infuse. Meanwhile, heat the oil and butter in a large saucepan. Add the onion and gently cook for 5 minutes, until softened. Stir in the garlic and ginger and cook for an additional 1 minute. Add the curry powder followed by the rice and stir until well coated.

Stir in the stock and saffron with its soaking liquid. Bring to a boil, then let simmer for 15 minutes.

Meanwhile, bring a saucepan of water to a boil. Carefully lower in the quail eggs and cook for 3 minutes. Remove from the pan and cool under cold running water, then shell and halve.

Break the salmon into flakes and add to the rice with the egg halves. Remove from the heat, cover, and let stand for 5 minutes to warm through. Gently stir in the crème fraîche or yogurt and season. Spoon onto plates and sprinkle with chopped parsley to serve.

For eggs with smoked salmon strips, bring a saucepan of water to a boil. Carefully lower in 4 hen eggs and cook for 4 minutes for a runny yolk. Transfer the eggs to egg cups. Wrap thin strips of smoked salmon around 8 long bread sticks and use to dunk in the eggs. **Total cooking time 10 minutes.**

roasted salmon with tartar sauce

Serves **4–6**
Total cooking time **30 minutes**

3 tablespoons **olive oil**
3 lb **thick piece of salmon**,
 cut into 2 fillets
1 **lemon**, sliced
handful of **mixed herbs**,
 finely chopped
salt

For the tartar sauce
⅓ cup **mayonnaise**
2 teaspoons drained **capers**,
 coarsely chopped
1 **scallion**, chopped
1 teaspoon **sugar**
1 teaspoon **whole-grain**
 mustard
lemon juice, to taste
handful of **dill**, chopped

To serve (optional)
buttered **new potatoes**
asparagus spears

Brush a large baking sheet with a little of the oil. Place 1 salmon fillet, skin side down, on the prepared sheet and season with a little salt. Top with the lemon slices and herbs. Season the other salmon fillet and place on top, skin side up.

Tie pieces of kitchen string around the salmon to secure. Drizzle with the remaining oil. Place in a preheated oven, at 425°F, for 25 minutes or until just cooked through.

Meanwhile, mix together the tartar sauce ingredients and put into a serving bowl.

Serve the fish with the tartar sauce alongside and some buttered new potatoes and asparagus, if desired.

For salmon with preserved lemon, mix together 1 teaspoon each ground cumin, paprika, and finely chopped preserved lemon, a handful of fresh cilantro, chopped, and 2 tablespoons olive oil. Make slits in the skin of 4 salmon fillets (about 5 oz each). Rub the spice mix all over and inside the slits. Set aside to marinate for 5–10 minutes. Heat a ridged grill pan until smoking hot. Cook the salmon, skin side down, for 4–5 minutes, then turn over and cook for an additional 3 minutes, until cooked through. Squeeze with a little lemon juice and serve with some couscous and a tomato salad. **Total cooking time 25 minutes.**

vegetarian

potato & celeriac soup

Serves **4**
Total cooking time **30 minutes**

1 **onion**, chopped
2 tablespoons **olive oil**
1 **garlic clove**, chopped
½ teaspoon **ground cumin**
½ teaspoon **ground coriander**
pinch of **dried red pepper
  flakes**
2 small **celeriac**, peeled and
  finely diced
2 **Yukon Gold** or white
  round potatoes, peeled
  and finely diced
4 cups hot **vegetable broth**
~~½ cup chopped~~ **fresh cilantro**
¼ cup **crème fraîche** or
  Greek yogurt, to serve
toasted **cumin seeds**,
  to garnish

Put the onion and olive oil into a saucepan with the garlic, cumin, ground coriander, and red pepper flakes. Sauté over medium heat for 1 minute.

Add the celeriac and potatoes, cover with the hot vegetable broth, and bring to a boil. Simmer for 15–20 minutes or until the vegetables are tender.

~~**Stir** in the fresh cilantro and~~ blend with an immersion blender until fairly smooth.

Serve in warm bowls with a dollop of crème fraîche or yogurt, sprinkled with toasted cumin seeds to garnish.

For spicy potato & celeriac stir-fry, heat ¼ cup vegetable oil in a large skillet or wok and add 1 chopped onion, 1 chopped garlic clove, 1 teaspoon each cumin and crushed coriander seeds, and 1 chopped red chile. Stir-fry over medium heat for 2–3 minutes. Add 1 large peeled and shredded potato and 1 large peeled and shredded celeriac. Stir-fry over high heat for 10–12 minutes or until the potato and celeriac are cooked through and tender. Remove from the heat and stir in a large handful of chopped fresh cilantro. Season and serve. **Total cooking time 20 minutes.**

squash with blue cheese fondue

Serves **4**

Total cooking time **30 minutes**

2 small **butternut squash** or
   4 **acorn squash** or **other**
   small squashes

1 tablespoon **olive oil**

1 cup **crème fraîche** or
   Greek yogurt

1 tablespoon **cornstarch**

8 oz **blue cheese**, crumbled
   (about 1⅓ cups)

handful of **thyme leaves**

salt and **black pepper**

Cut the squash in half and trim a thin slice off the rounded back of each half so that they will sit securely, cut side up. Scoop out and discard the seeds and fibers, then score the cut surface of the squash in a crisscross pattern. Drizzle the oil over the squash and season. Arrange on a baking sheet and cook in a preheated oven, at 450°F, for 15 minutes, until tender.

Meanwhile, mix together the crème fraîche or yogurt and cornstarch, then mash in the blue cheese with a fork and add plenty of black pepper.

Divide the mixture among the cavities of the squash halves, sprinkle with the thyme leaves, and return to the oven for an additional 10 minutes, until the filling is golden and bubbling.

For squash & blue cheese frittata, heat ¼ cup olive oil in a large, nonstick skillet. Add 1 sliced red onion and 1 small butternut squash, peeled, seeded, and diced, and cook for 5 minutes, until softened. Meanwhile, beat 5 eggs with 2 finely chopped sage leaves and season well. Reduce the heat to low, then pour the eggs into the pan. Crumble 2 oz blue cheese (about ⅓ cup) over the top, then cook gently for 10–15 minutes, until the eggs are just set. **Total cooking time 20 minutes.**

tomato, basil & mozzarella salad

Serves **4**

Total cooking time **20 minutes**

3 tablespoons **extra virgin olive oil**

juice of ½ **lemon**

1 teaspoon **honey**

1 teaspoon **mustard**

1 **garlic clove**, crushed

7 **ripe tomatoes** (about 1¾ lb)

2 (8 oz) packages **mozzarella cheese**, sliced

10–12 **basil leaves**, torn

black pepper

Whisk together the olive oil, lemon juice, honey, mustard, garlic, and some black pepper in a bowl.

Put the tomatoes into a large bowl and pour over enough boiling water to cover. Let stand for 30 seconds, then drain and refresh under cold running water. Peel off the skins and slice the tomatoes.

Layer the tomatoes with the slices of mozzarella and torn basil leaves in individual bowls or one large serving bowl.

Drizzle with the dressing and let stand for 5 minutes before serving.

For tomato & mozzarella tart, roll out 1 sheet of ready-to-bake chilled puff pastry on a lightly floured work surface to 10 inches square. Place on a baking sheet and score a 1 inch border around the pastry. Bake in a preheated oven, at 400°F, for 10 minutes, until golden. Slice 4 ripe tomatoes (about 1¼ lb) and 1 (8 oz) package mozzarella cheese and place, slightly overlapping, within the border. Top with 10–12 basil leaves and sprinkle with 2 tablespoons pine nuts. Bake for an additional 10–12 minutes, until the cheese is melted and the pastry is golden. Meanwhile, whisk together 2 tablespoons olive oil and 1 tablespoon balsamic vinegar and toss with 2½ cups arugula. Serve with the baked tart. **Total cooking time 30 minutes.**

roasted chickpeas with spinach

Serves **4**
Total cooking time **20 minutes**

1 (15 oz) can **chickpeas (garbanzo beans)**, rinsed and drained
3 tablespoons **olive** or **vegetable oil**
1 teaspoon **cumin seeds**
1 teaspoon **paprika**
½ **red onion**, thinly sliced
3 **ripe tomatoes**, coarsely chopped
3½ cups **baby spinach**
3½ oz **feta cheese**, crumbled (about ⅔ cup, optional)
2 tablespoons **lemon juice**
salt and **black pepper**
lemon wedges, to garnish

Mix the chickpeas (garbanzo beans) in a bowl with 1 tablespoon of the oil, the cumin seeds, and the paprika, and season with salt and black pepper. Transfer to a large, nonstick roasting pan and roast in a preheated oven, at 425°F, for 12–15 minutes, until nutty and golden.

Meanwhile, put the onion and tomatoes into a large bowl with the spinach and toss gently to combine. Pile onto 4 serving plates.

Remove the chickpeas from the oven and sprinkle them over the spinach salad. Sprinkle with the feta, if using, and drizzle each plate with the lemon juice and remaining olive oil. Garnish with lemon wedges and serve immediately.

For chickpea & spinach salad, toss 1 (15 oz) can chickpeas (garbanzo beans), rinsed and drained, with 3 tablespoons olive or vegetable oil and 1 teaspoon each cumin seeds and paprika. Season with salt and black pepper. Put into a large skillet and heat for 2–3 minutes, stirring occasionally, until hot and fragrant. Remove from the heat, toss with ½ red onion, thinly sliced, and 3 ripe tomatoes, coarsely chopped, and fold into 3½ cups baby spinach, torn. Pile onto serving plates and serve with 3½ oz crumbled feta cheese (about ⅔ cup), if desired. **Total cooking time 10 minutes.**

broccoli & blue cheese soufflés

Serves **4**

Total cooking time **30 minutes**

handful of **fine fresh white bread crumbs**

4 cups **broccoli florets**

4 tablespoons **butter**, plus extra, melted, for greasing

⅓ cup **all-purpose flour**

1¼ cups **milk**

1 teaspoon **smoked paprika**

freshly grated **nutmeg**

4 **extra-large eggs**, separated

3½ oz (¾ cup) **creamy blue cheese**, crumbled

salt and **black pepper**

Brush four 1¼ cup ramekins with melted butter. Sprinkle with bread crumbs to coat the bottom and sides.

Blanch the broccoli in boiling water until almost tender, then pulse in a food processor or blender until smooth.

Melt the butter in a saucepan, add the flour, and cook for 2 minutes. Gradually add the milk, stirring continuously, and bring to a boil. Boil for 2 minutes, until thick.

Remove from the heat and stir in the spices and egg yolks. Season well, then stir in the pureed broccoli and the cheese.

Whisk the egg whites in a large, grease-free bowl until stiff. Using a metal spoon, carefully fold the egg whites into the broccoli and cheese mixture.

Pour into the ramekins, almost up to the rim. Run your finger around the inside edge of each ramekin to help the soufflés rise straight up. Bake on a hot baking sheet in a preheated oven, at 400°F, for 8–10 minutes or until risen. Serve immediately.

For thick broccoli & blue cheese soup, put 1 (18½ oz) can or container of good-quality vegetable soup in a saucepan with 6 cups finely chopped broccoli florets and bring to a boil. Let simmer, uncovered, for 5–6 minutes, then blend with an immersion blender until fairly smooth. Stir in 1 cup heavy cream and 3½ oz crumbled creamy blue cheese (about ¾ cup). Season and serve in warm bowls with crusty bread. **Total cooking time 10 minutes.**

~~wild~~ mushroom tart

Serves **4**
Total cooking time **30 minutes**

1 sheet **ready-to-bake rolled dough piecrust**
2 tablespoons **olive oil**
1 **red onion**, sliced
12 oz **mushrooms**, ~~including a variety of~~ **wild** ~~and~~ **cremini**, ~~trimmed and sliced~~
2 **eggs**, beaten
½ cup **mascarpone cheese**
1 teaspoon **thyme leaves**
2 teaspoons **whole-grain mustard**
½ cup grated **Parmesan cheese**
black pepper

Use the dough to line a 9 inch tart pan. Chill while you make the filling.

Heat the olive oil in a skillet and cook the onion and mushrooms for 5 minutes, stirring frequently.

Meanwhile, beat together the eggs, mascarpone, and thyme leaves in a bowl and season with black pepper.

Add the onion and mushrooms to the egg mixture and mix well.

Spread the mustard over the bottom of the tart shell. Pour in the filling and level with the back of a spoon.

Sprinkle with the grated Parmesan and bake in a preheated oven, at 400°F, for 20 minutes, until golden. Slice into generous pieces and serve hot or cold.

For mushroom & Taleggio bruschetta, heat 2 tablespoons olive oil in a skillet and sauté 4 oz wild mushrooms, trimmed, with 1 crushed garlic clove for 4–5 minutes. Stir in 1 tablespoon chopped parsley. Toast 8 slices of large baguette on both sides. Top each slice of bread with the mushroom mixture and then a slice of Taleggio cheese. Cook under a preheated hot broiler for 1–2 minutes, until the cheese is bubbling. Serve warm. **Total cooking time 10 minutes.**

pea & mint risotto

Serves **4**

Total cooking time **30 minutes**

1 tablespoon **olive oil**
2 **shallots**, finely diced
2 cups **risotto rice**
½ cup **white wine**
3¾–4 cups hot **vegetable broth**
⅔ cup **fresh** or **frozen peas**, defrosted
small handful of **mint leaves**, chopped
3 tablespoons **butter**
½ cup grated **Parmesan cheese**
salt and **black pepper**

Heat the oil in a large saucepan and sauté the shallots for 2–3 minutes, until softened.

Stir in the rice and cook, stirring, until the edges of the grains look translucent. Pour in the wine and cook for 1–2 minutes, until it is absorbed.

Add a ladleful of the hot vegetable broth and cook, stirring continuously, until it has all been absorbed. Repeat with the remaining hot broth, adding a ladleful at a time, until the rice is al dente.

Stir in the peas, mint, butter, and half the Parmesan, season with salt and black pepper, and cook for an additional 2–3 minutes.

Serve sprinkled with the remaining grated Parmesan.

For pea & mint pasta salad, cook 8 oz fresh penne according to the package directions, until al dente, then drain and refresh under cold running water. Meanwhile, cook 2 cups frozen peas in boiling water for 3–4 minutes, then drain and refresh under cold running water. Toss the pasta and peas with 8 cherry tomatoes, halved, 1 tablespoon chopped mint leaves, 4 oz chopped mozzarella cheese, and 2 tablespoons pitted black ripe olives in a salad bowl. Add 4 cups baby spinach and 3–4 tablespoons Italian salad dressing and toss together gently. **Total cooking time 10 minutes.**

potato & onion pizza

Serves **4**

Total cooking time **30 minutes**

2⅓ cups **all-purpose flour**

2¼ teaspoons **dry active yeast**

1½ teaspoons **sugar**

1 teaspoon **salt**

¾ cup warm **water**

3 tablespoons **olive oil**, plus extra for oiling

½ cup **crème fraîche** or **ricotta cheese**

8 oz unpeeled **new potatoes**, thinly sliced on a mandoline

½ **onion**, thinly sliced on a mandoline

2 teaspoons **dried thyme**

1 cup shredded **Swiss** or **cheddar cheese**

12 **black ripe olives** (optional)

cracked black pepper

Mix together the flour, yeast, sugar, and salt in a large bowl. Make a well in the center and pour in the measured water and 2 tablespoons of the oil. Combine to make a soft dough, then roll out to a rectangle about 14 x 10 inches. Transfer to a lightly oiled baking sheet and cook in a preheated oven, at 400°F, for 5 minutes or until just beginning to brown.

Spoon ¼ cup of the crème fraîche or ricotta cheese over the pizza crust. Top with the slices of potato and onion, then sprinkle with the thyme and shredded cheese. Drizzle the remaining oil over the pizza and return to the oven. Increase the temperature to 425°F and bake for about 15 minutes, until golden.

Cut the pizza into slices, sprinkle with the olives, if using, and top with the remaining crème fraîche or ricotta. Season with cracked black pepper and serve hot.

For creamy potato & onion gnocchi, heat
2 tablespoons olive oil in a skillet, and cook 1 chopped onion and 2 chopped garlic cloves for 7–8 minutes. Meanwhile, cook 1 (16 oz) package gnocchi according to the package directions, then drain. Add 1¾ cups crème fraîche or heavy cream, 1 teaspoon thyme, and 1 cup shredded Swiss or cheddar cheese to the onion mixture, and stir for 1 minute. Season generously and stir in the gnocchi. Spoon into 4 bowls and serve immediately, with extra cheese, if desired. **Total cooking time 15 minutes.**

black bean broccoli & mushroom

Serves **4**
Total cooking time **20 minutes**

1 tablespoon **sunflower oil**
¾ inch piece of **fresh ginger root**, peeled and sliced into matchsticks
3 cups small **broccoli florets**
8 oz **shiitake mushrooms**, trimmed
6 **scallions**, sliced into ¾ inch lengths
1 **red bell pepper**, cored, seeded, and sliced
1¼ cups **vegetable broth**
1 (16 oz) package **fresh egg noodles**
2 tablespoons **light soy sauce**
1 tablespoon **cornstarch**, mixed to a paste with 2 tablespoons water

For the sauce
1 tablespoon **fermented black beans**, rinsed well
1 tablespoon **light soy sauce**
2 **garlic cloves**, crushed
1 **red chile,** seeded and chopped
1 tablespoon **Chinese rice wine**

Put all the ingredients for the black bean sauce into a food processor or blender, process until fairly smooth, and set aside.

Heat a wok over high heat and add the oil. When smoking, add the ginger and stir-fry for a few seconds, then add the broccoli and stir-fry for an additional 2–3 minutes.

Add the mushrooms, scallions, and red bell pepper and stir-fry for 2–3 minutes.

Stir in the black bean sauce and vegetable broth and bring to a simmer. Cook for 2–3 minutes, until tender.

Meanwhile, cook the noodles according to the package directions, drain, and keep warm.

Add the soy sauce, mix in the cornstarch paste, and cook to thicken for 1 minute. Serve immediately with the egg noodles.

For broccoli, mushroom & black bean stir-fry, heat 1 tablespoon vegetable oil in a large wok, add 4 cups broccoli florets, 10 oz trimmed and sliced shiitake mushrooms, and 6 sliced scallions, and stir-fry over high heat for 3–4 minutes. Add ⅓–½ cup store-bought black bean stir-fry sauce and ½ cup water and stir-fry over high heat for 3–4 minutes. Serve the stir-fry over noodles. **Total cooking time 15 minutes.**

mushroom & herb crepes

Serves **4**

Total cooking time **30 minutes**

2 tablespoons **butter**, plus extra for greasing

10 oz **small cremini mushrooms**, trimmed and sliced

6 **scallions**, finely sliced

2 **garlic cloves**, crushed

1 (16 oz) jar or can **four cheese alfredo** or **cheese sauce**

1 (12 oz) package **baby spinach**

¼ cup finely chopped **parsley**

2 tablespoons finely chopped **tarragon**

8 **cooked crepes** (prepared from a pancake mix, adding extra water for a thin batter)

½ cup grated **Parmesan cheese**

salt and **black pepper**

lettuce, to serve

Heat the butter in a large, nonstick skillet, add the mushrooms, scallions, and garlic, and sauté over high heat for 6–7 minutes.

Stir in half the alfredo or cheese sauce and heat until just bubbling. Add the spinach and cook for 1 minute, until just wilted. Remove from the heat, stir in the chopped herbs, and season.

Take 1 crepe and spoon one-eighth of the filling down the center. Carefully roll up the crepe and place in a shallow, greased gratin dish. Repeat with the remaining crepes. Drizzle the remaining cheese sauce over the crepes, sprinkle with the grated Parmesan, and season. Cook under a preheated medium-hot broiler for 3–4 minutes, until piping hot and turning golden.

Remove from the broiler and serve with lettuce.

For creamy mushroom spaghetti, cook 12 oz quick-cook spaghetti according to the package directions until al dente. Meanwhile, process 12 oz cremini mushrooms, trimmed, in a food processor or blender with 1 (16 oz) jar or can four cheese alfredo sauce or cheese sauce, then transfer to a large saucepan and bring to a boil. Simmer for 2–3 minutes, then stir in ¼ cup chopped tarragon. Drain the pasta, add to the mushroom mixture, and mix well, then season and serve immediately. **Total cooking time 10 minutes.**

quinoa & feta with roasted veggies

Serves **4**
Total cooking time **30 minutes**

1 **red bell pepper**, cored,
  seeded, and cut into chunks
1 **yellow bell pepper**, cored,
  seeded, and cut into chunks
1 **red onion**, cut into wedges
2 **zucchini**, sliced
2 **garlic cloves**, unpeeled
¼ **butternut squash**, peeled,
  seeded, and cut into chunks
2 tablespoons **olive oil**
1 cup **quinoa**
8 oz **feta cheese**, crumbled
  (about 1½ cups)
small handful of **parsley**,
  coarsely chopped
salt and **black pepper**

Put the bell peppers, onion, zucchini, garlic, and squash into a roasting pan and toss with the oil. Roast in a preheated oven, at 400°F, for 25 minutes or until tender and browned.

Meanwhile, cook the quinoa in a saucepan of boiling water for 8–9 minutes or according to the package directions. Drain and refresh under cold running water, then set aside.

Remove the vegetables from the oven. Squeeze the flesh from the garlic cloves into the vegetables. Season well with salt and black pepper.

Stir the quinoa, feta, and parsley into the roasted vegetables and serve.

For quinoa, feta & raw vegetable salad, cook ¼ cup quinoa in a saucepan of boiling water for 8–9 minutes or according to the package directions. Meanwhile, in a large bowl, mix together 2 large tomatoes, diced, ½ cucumber, diced, a small bunch each of parsley and mint, chopped, 1 small red onion, diced, 1 cup shredded snow peas, and 1 cored, seeded, and diced red bell pepper. Drain and refresh the quinoa under cold running water, then stir into the salad ingredients with 2–3 tablespoons store-bought vinaigrette and 3½ oz crumbled feta (about ⅔ cup). **Total cooking time 15 minutes.**

halloumi & zucchini with salsa

Serves **4**

Total cooking time **15 minutes**

2 tablespoons **olive oil**

8 oz **baby zucchini**, halved
   lengthwise

8 oz **halloumi cheese**
   or **Muenster cheese**,
   thickly sliced

salt and **black pepper**

For the salsa

2 **roasted red bell peppers
   from a jar**, drained and
   finely chopped

1 **garlic clove**, crushed

1 **red chile,** seeded and
   finely chopped

finely grated zest and juice
   of ½ **lemon**

2 tablespoons **extra virgin
   olive oil**

handful of chopped **mint**

Heat half the olive oil in a large skillet. Add the zucchini and cook for 2 minutes, then turn over and cook for an additional 1 minute, until golden. Season, remove from the pan, and keep warm.

Add the remaining olive oil to the pan, followed by the cheese. Cook the cheese for 1–2 minutes on each side, until golden.

Meanwhile, mix together all the ingredients for the salsa in a bowl.

Divide the zucchini and halloumi among serving plates and spoon the salsa over the top to serve.

For roasted halloumi & zucchini-stuffed peppers, cut 4 red or yellow bell peppers in half lengthwise, remove the cores and seeds, and place on a baking sheet, cut side up. Drizzle 1 tablespoon olive oil over them and season well. Put into a preheated oven, at 400°F, for 10 minutes. Meanwhile, shred 2 small zucchini and mix with 1 beaten egg and 8 oz ricotta cheese (about 1 cup). Season and spoon into the bell peppers. Top the filling with a slice of halloumi or mozzarella cheese and return to the oven for an additional 10–15 minutes, until golden and just set. **Total cooking time 30 minutes.**

zingy ~~wild~~ mushroom rice

Serves **4**

Total cooking time **30 minutes**

2 tablespoons **butter**

1 tablespoon **olive oil**

8 oz ~~wild~~ **mushrooms**, trimmed and coarsely chopped

1 **onion**, finely chopped

2 **garlic cloves**, crushed

1⅓ cups **mixed wild and basmati rice**

3 cups **vegetable broth**

finely grated zest and juice of 1 **lemon**

2 **scallions**, chopped

large handful of chopped **parsley**

½ **red chile**, chopped

salt and **black pepper**

Heat the butter and oil in a large, heavy saucepan. Add the mushrooms and cook for 3 minutes, until golden, then remove from the pan and set aside. Add the onion to the pan and cook for 5 minutes, until softened, then stir in the garlic. Add the rice and stir until coated in the oil, then pour in the broth.

Bring to a boil, then reduce the heat and simmer for about 15 minutes, or according to the package directions, until most of the liquid has been absorbed. Return the mushrooms to the pan, cover, and cook gently for 5 minutes or until the rice is tender. Season and stir in the remaining ingredients before serving.

For mushroom & rice cakes, heat 1 tablespoon butter and 1 tablespoon olive oil in a nonstick skillet. Add 1 crushed garlic clove and 5 oz mushrooms, trimmed and finely chopped, and cook for 5 minutes. Remove from the pan and let cool for a few minutes. Mix the mushrooms with 1 egg yolk, 1½ cups cooked rice, ¼ cup grated Parmesan cheese, the finely grated zest of ½ lemon, a pinch of dried red pepper flakes, and a handful of chopped parsley. Season to taste and shape into small cakes with your hands, then lightly coat with all-purpose flour. Heat a little more oil in the skillet, then cook the cakes for 3 minutes on each side, until golden and cooked through. Serve with a tomato salad. **Total cooking time 20 minutes.**

pizza fiorentina

Serves **4**

Total cooking time **15 minutes**

4 cups **baby spinach**

4 large **wheat tortillas** or **flatbreads**

⅔ cup **tomato sauce**

4 oz **mozzarella cheese**, sliced

4 **eggs**

¼ cup grated **Parmesan cheese**

Put the spinach into a strainer and pour over boiling water until wilted, then squeeze thoroughly to remove excess water.

Arrange the tortillas or flatbreads on 4 pizza pans. Spoon the tomato sauce over them, then sprinkle with the spinach. Arrange the mozzarella on top, then crack an egg into the center of each tortilla or flatbread.

Sprinkle the Parmesan over the pizzas, then place in a preheated oven, at 425°F, for 5–7 minutes, until the egg whites are just set.

For baked tomato, spinach & tortilla, put 2 (6 oz) packages baby spinach into a strainer and pour over boiling water until wilted, then squeeze thoroughly to remove excess water. Mix with 1 (8 oz) package ricotta cheese (about 1 cup) and 3 oz crumbled feta cheese (about ½ cup). Divide among 8 small tortillas or flatbreads, roll up to enclose the filling, and place in a lightly greased ovenproof dish, seam side down. Pour 2 cups tomato sauce over the top and sprinkle with 4 oz sliced mozzarella cheese and ½ cup shredded cheddar cheese. Cook in a preheated oven, at 375°F, for 20 minutes, until bubbling and golden. **Total cooking time 30 minutes.**

spicy paneer with peas

Serves **4**

Total cooking time **25 minutes**

2 tablespoons **vegetable oil**

8 oz **paneer** or **firm tofu**,
  diced

1 **onion**, finely chopped

2 **garlic cloves**, chopped

2 teaspoons finely grated
  fresh ginger root

1 teaspoon **ground coriander**

1 teaspoon **paprika**

1 teaspoon **tomato paste**

½ cup hot **vegetable broth**

4 oz **green beans**, trimmed
  (about 1 cup)

1 cup **frozen peas**

1 **tomato**, chopped

1 teaspoon **garam masala**

salt and **black pepper**

chapattis or **other flatbreads**,
  to serve

Heat half the oil in a large skillet. Add the paneer or tofu, season well, and cook for 3–4 minutes, until golden all over. Remove from the pan and set aside. Add the remaining oil to the pan, then add the onion. Sauté for 5 minutes, until softened, then add the garlic and ginger and sauté for an additional 1 minute. Add the spices and cook for 30 seconds.

Stir in the tomato paste and broth, then return the paneer to the pan along with the green beans. Season, cover, and simmer for 5 minutes. Add the peas and tomatoes and cook for an additional 3 minutes, then stir in the garam masala.

Divide among warm bowls and serve with chapattis or other flatbreads.

For spicy paneer & tomato skewers, cut 8 oz paneer or firm tofu into large cubes. Mix 1 teaspoon garam masala with ½ teaspoon ground cumin, a pinch of ground turmeric, a handful of chopped fresh cilantro, and 2 tablespoons vegetable oil. Toss with the paneer, then thread onto metal skewers with some whole cherry tomatoes. Season. Heat a ridged grill pan until smoking hot, then cook the skewers for 3–5 minutes, turning once, until lightly charred. Serve with green salad and chapattis or other flatbreads. **Total cooking time 10 minutes.**

lemon & herb risotto

Serves **4**

Total cooking time **30 minutes**

1 tablespoon **olive oil**

3 **shallots**, finely chopped

2 **garlic cloves**, finely chopped

½ **head of celery**, finely chopped

1 **zucchini**, finely diced

1 **carrot**, peeled and finely diced

1½ cups **risotto rice**

5 cups hot **vegetable broth**

good handful of **mixed herbs**, such as tarragon, parsley, chives, dill

1 stick (4 oz) **butter**

1 tablespoon finely grated **lemon zest**

1 cup freshly grated **Parmesan cheese**

salt and **black pepper**

Heat the oil in a large saucepan, add the shallots, garlic, celery, zucchini, and carrot, and sauté for 4 minutes or until the vegetables have softened. Add the rice and cook, stirring, for 2–3 minutes.

Add a ladleful of the hot broth followed by half the herbs, season well, and cook, stirring continuously, until it has all been absorbed. Repeat with the remaining hot broth, adding a ladleful at a time, until the rice is al dente.

Remove from the heat and gently stir in the remaining herbs, the butter, lemon zest, and Parmesan. Place the lid on the pan and let stand for 2–3 minutes, during which time it will become creamy and oozy. Serve immediately, sprinkled with black pepper.

For lemon & vegetable rice, heat 1 tablespoon olive oil in a large skillet, add 2 chopped shallots, 2 chopped garlic cloves, and 1 (12 oz) package stir-fry vegetables, and stir-fry briefly. Add 2 (9 oz) packages microwavable rice and the finely grated zest and juice of 1 small lemon. Stir-fry for 5–6 minutes or until piping hot. Serve immediately. **Total cooking time 10 minutes.**

baked zucchini & ricotta

Serves **4**

Total cooking time **30 minutes**

butter, for greasing

2 **zucchini**

2 cups **fresh white bread crumbs**

1 (8 oz) package **ricotta cheese** (about 1 cup)

1 cup grated **Parmesan cheese**

2 **eggs**

1 **garlic clove**, crushed

handful of chopped **basil**

salt and **black pepper**

Grease 8 cups of 1–2 large muffin pans. Use a vegetable peeler to make 16 long ribbons of zucchini and set aside. Shred the remainder of the zucchini and squeeze to remove any excess moisture.

Mix the shredded zucchini with the remaining ingredients and season well. Arrange 2 zucchini ribbons in a cross shape in each cup of the muffin pan. Spoon in the filling and fold over the overhanging zucchini ends.

Place in a preheated oven, at 375°F, for 15–20 minutes or until golden and cooked through. Turn out onto serving plates.

For mushrooms stuffed with zucchini & ricotta, brush a little olive oil over 4 large portobello mushrooms, trimmed, and place on a baking sheet, stem side up. Shred 1 zucchini and squeeze to remove any excess moisture, then mix with 1 (8 oz) package ricotta cheese (about 1 cup), 4 drained and chopped sun-dried tomatoes in oil, and ¼ cup chopped, pitted black ripe olives. Season and spoon onto the mushrooms, then sprinkle with ¼ cup grated Parmesan cheese. Place in a preheated oven, at 400°F, for 15 minutes, until golden and cooked through. Serve with ciabatta rolls. **Total cooking time 20 minutes.**

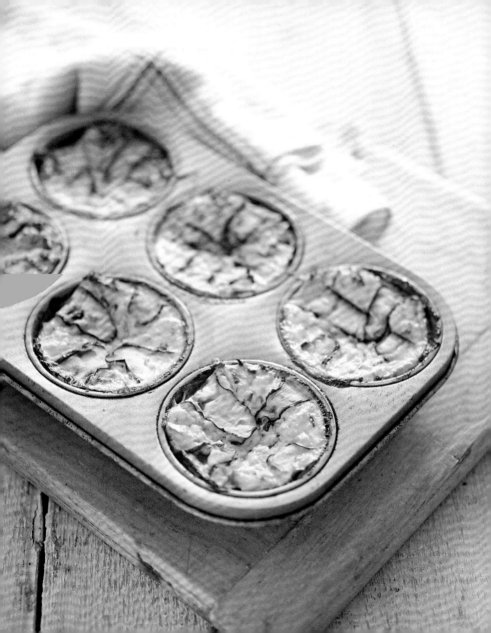

creamy asparagus cappellacci

Serves **4**

Total cooking time **20 minutes**

1 lb **cappellacci, bow ties**, or
   other pasta shapes
1 bunch of **asparagus spears**,
   trimmed
1 tablespoon **butter**
1 **garlic clove**, sliced
5 oz **mixed wild mushrooms,**
   trimmed and halved if large
⅓ cup **crème fraîche** or
   heavy cream
salt and **black pepper**
Parmesan cheese shavings,
   to serve

Cook the pasta according to the package directions until al dente. Add the asparagus 3 minutes before the end of the cooking time and cook until just tender.

Meanwhile, heat the butter in a skillet, add the garlic, and cook for 1 minute, then stir in the mushrooms and cook for 5 minutes, until soft and golden. Stir in the crème fraîche or heavy cream.

Drain the pasta and asparagus, reserving a little of the cooking water, and return to the pan. Stir through the mushroom sauce and season, adding a little cooking water to loosen, if needed. Spoon into serving bowls and serve sprinkled with Parmesan shavings.

For asparagus linguine with lemon carbonara sauce, cook 1 lb linguine according to the package directions until al dente, adding asparagus spears, trimmed, 3 minutes before the end of the cooking time. Meanwhile, mix together 1 egg, 3 tablespoons crème fraîche or heavy cream, and a good squeeze of lemon juice in a bowl. Drain the pasta and asparagus and return to the pan. Toss through the egg sauce and serve immediately. **Total cooking time 15 minutes.**

tricolore couscous salad

Serves **4**

Total cooking time **20 minutes**

1 cup **couscous**

1¼ cups hot **vegetable broth**
or **boiling water**

16 **cherry tomatoes**, halved

2 **avocados**, peeled, pitted,
and chopped

4 oz **mozzarella cheese**,
chopped

handful of **arugula**

For the dressing

2 tablespoons **green pesto**

1 tablespoon **lemon juice**

¼ cup **extra virgin olive oil**

salt and **black pepper**

Mix the couscous and broth or boiling water together in a bowl, then cover with a plate and let stand for 10 minutes.

Make the dressing. Mix the pesto with the lemon juice and season, then gradually mix in the oil. Pour the dressing over the couscous and mix with a fork.

Add the tomatoes, avocados, and mozzarella to the couscous, mix well, then lightly stir in the arugula.

For cherry tomato, avocado & mozzarella pasta, finely chop 2 cups cherry tomatoes, 2 peeled and pitted avocados, 2 cups arugula, and 8 oz mozzarella cheese. Put into a bowl with ⅓ cup green pesto and 2 tablespoons olive oil. Season and stir to mix well. Let stand at room temperature for 15 minutes for the flavors to develop. Meanwhile, cook 12 oz spaghetti according to the package directions until al dente. Drain the pasta and transfer to a wide serving dish. Add the cherry tomato mixture, toss to mix well, and serve. **Total cooking time 25 minutes.**

gnocchi with spinach & walnuts

Serves **4**

Total cooking time **30 minutes**

1 tablespoon **olive oil**

8 cups **baby spinach**

1 (16 oz) package **gnocchi**

1 cup **crème fraîche** or **heavy cream**

½ teaspoon **whole-grain mustard**

¾ cup shredded **cheddar cheese**

¼ cup grated **Pecorino cheese**

¼ cup **walnut pieces**

Heat the olive oil in a skillet and cook the spinach briefly just until it has wilted.

Cook the gnocchi in a saucepan of boiling water according to the package directions. Drain.

Put the crème fraîche or heavy cream and mustard into a saucepan, stir in about half each of the cheeses, and cook for 2–3 minutes, then stir in the spinach and gnocchi to heat through. Stir in the walnuts.

Pour into an ovenproof dish and sprinkle with the remaining cheese. Cook under a preheated hot broiler for 3–4 minutes, until golden and serve.

For cheesy spinach grits with creamy mushrooms, heat 2 tablespoons olive oil in a saucepan and sauté 8 oz cremini mushrooms, trimmed and chopped, with 2 chopped shallots and 2 chopped garlic cloves for 5 minutes. Stir in 3 tablespoons crème fraîche or heavy cream with ½ teaspoon whole-grain mustard and ¼ cup chopped toasted walnuts. Meanwhile, bring 5 cups vegetable broth to a boil in a separate saucepan, pour in 2 cups instant grits or polenta, and cook, stirring continuously, for 5–6 minutes, until thick and creamy. Remove from the heat and stir in 3½ oz chopped Fontina cheese and 2 cups coarsely chopped baby spinach. Divide the grits among 4 warm bowls, spoon the creamy mushrooms over the top, and serve sprinkled with 2 tablespoons grated Pecorino cheese. **Total cooking time 20 minutes.**

desserts

quick mini lemon meringue pies

Serves **4**
Total cooking time **20 minutes**

4 **baked individual pastry
  shells**
¾ cup **lemon curd**
1 **egg white**
¼ cup **sugar**

Fill each pastry shell with 3 tablespoons of the lemon curd.

Whisk the egg white in a clean, grease-free bowl, until it forms soft peaks and hold its shape. Gradually whisk in the sugar, a little at a time, until the mixture is thick and glossy.

Pipe the meringue mixture in swirls over the lemon curd. Place the pies on a baking sheet and bake on the top shelf of a preheated oven, at 400°F, for 5–6 minutes or until the meringue is just beginning to brown. Let cool slightly and serve.

For lemon meringue & blueberry desserts, coarsely crush 2 store-bought meringue nests and put into the bottom of 4 dessert bowls. Whip 1 cup heavy cream until it forms soft peaks and then stir in ½ cup lemon curd to create a marbled effect. Spoon the curd and cream mixture over the crushed meringue and top each with 3 tablespoons blueberries. **Total cooking time 10 minutes.**

blackberry & apple cranachan

Serves **4**

Total cooking time **20 minutes**

4 teaspoons **rolled oats**
8 teaspoons **sugar**
2 tablespoons **butter**
1 **crisp, sweet apple**, peeled,
  cored, and coarsely grated
1 cup **vanilla yogurt**
½ teaspoon **ground
  cinnamon**
1 tablespoon **whiskey**
3 cups **blackberries,**
  plus extra to decorate

Put a small skillet over medium-high heat. Add the oats and cook for 1 minute, then add 1 tablespoon of the sugar.

Dry-fry, stirring for 2–3 minutes or until the oats are lightly browned, then transfer to a piece of parchment paper and let cool.

Meanwhile, heat a nonstick skillet over high heat, add the butter, and sauté the apple for 3–4 minutes. When the apple begins to soften, add 4 teaspoons of the remaining sugar and cook until lightly browned. Let cool.

Mix together the yogurt, cinnamon, the remaining sugar, and the whiskey. Stir in the blackberries, crushing them slightly.

Layer the blackberry mixture with the apple in 4 dessert glasses. Top with extra blackberries, sprinkle with the oat mixture, and serve.

For warm blackberry & cinnamon compote, heat 4⅓ cups blackberries (about 1¼ lb) with 1 teaspoon ground cinnamon, ¼ cup sugar, and a squeeze of lemon juice in a saucepan and bring to a boil. Cook for 5–6 minutes or until the berries have broken down and the mixture has thickened. Serve warm over scoops of ice cream or with vanilla yogurt. **Total cooking time 10 minutes.**

lime cheesecake

Serves **4–6**
Total cooking time **30 minutes**

2 cups crushed **graham
  crackers**
1 stick (4 oz) **butter**, melted
finely grated zest of **1 lime** and
   1½ tablespoons juice
1¼ cups **cream cheese**
¾ cup **confectioners' sugar**,
   sifted
lime slices, halved, to decorate

Put the crushed cookies into a bowl and stir in the melted butter until well coated. Line the sides of a loose-bottom 8 inch cake pan with plastic wrap, then replace the bottom and press the cookie mixture evenly over the bottom of the pan. Chill in the refrigerator while making the filling.

Put the lime zest and juice into a clean bowl with the cream cheese and confectioners' sugar, and beat until smooth.

Spoon the filling over the chilled crust and smooth down with a spatula. Decorate with slices of lime. Return to the refrigerator for 20 minutes.

Remove the cheesecake from the pan and gently peel away the plastic wrap. Cut into slices and serve.

For lime cheesecake sandwiches, put the finely grated zest of 1 lime and 1½ tablespoons lime juice into a bowl with 1¼ cups cream cheese and ¾ cup confectioners' sugar, and beat until smooth. Cover and chill the cheesecake filling in the refrigerator for 15 minutes. Divide the mixture among 8 graham crackers, then top each one with a second cracker. Serve immediately. **Total cooking time 25 minutes.**

banana & caramel layers

Serves **4**
Total cooking time **20 minutes**

6 **graham crackers**
2 large **bananas**
4 tablespoons **butter**
¼ cup packed **dark
   brown sugar**
⅔ cup **heavy cream**
1 cup **crème fraîche** or
   Greek yogurt
grated **semisweet chocolate**,
   to decorate

Put the cookies into a plastic bag and smash with a rolling pin to form fine crumbs. Divide among 4 tall serving glasses and use to line each bottom.

Mash 1 of the bananas and divide among the 4 glasses, spooning on top of the cookie crumbs.

Melt the butter in a small saucepan, add the sugar, and heat over medium heat, stirring well, until the sugar has dissolved. Add the heavy cream and cook gently for 1–2 minutes, until the mixture is thick. Remove from the heat and let cool for 1 minute, then spoon on top of the mashed banana.

Slice the second banana and arrange on top of the caramel, then spoon the crème fraîche or yogurt over the banana. Decorate with grated semisweet chocolate before serving.

For banana, caramel & date desserts, lightly whip 1 ¼ cups heavy cream in a large bowl. Crumble in 4 store-bought meringue nests, then fold in 4 sliced bananas and a handful of chopped pitted dates. Swirl over ¼ cup store-bought dulce de leche (caramel sauce). Spoon into 4 serving dishes, sprinkle with a handful of pecans, and drizzle with a little more sauce. **Total cooking time 10 minutes.**

poached apricots with amaretti

Serves **4**

Total cooking time **30 minutes**

10–12 **apricots** (about 1 lb),
   halved and pitted
¼ cup packed **light brown
   sugar**
1 **vanilla bean**, split
   lengthwise
⅓ cup **water**
finely grated zest of 1 **lemon**
1 cup **crème fraîche** or
   Greek yogurt

For the amaretti
1 **egg white**
¾ cup **ground almonds**
½ cup **sugar**

Put the apricots into a heavy saucepan with the brown sugar, vanilla bean, and measured water and bring to a boil. Reduce the heat, cover, and simmer for 15 minutes, until the apricots are tender yet just retaining their shape.

Meanwhile, for the amaretti, whisk the egg white in a grease-free bowl until stiff. Fold in the ground almonds and sugar until well mixed. Line a baking sheet with parchment paper and spoon tablespoonfuls of the mixture onto the lined sheet, well spaced apart.

Bake in a preheated oven, at 375°F, for 10 minutes, until just beginning to brown. Let cool on the paper for 5 minutes, then carefully peel away from the paper and transfer to a wire rack.

Mix the lemon zest into the crème fraîche or yogurt.

Remove the vanilla bean from the apricots and spoon into serving dishes. Serve with the lemon cream and soft amaretti.

For apricot & peach pavlovas, spoon 2 tablespoons Greek yogurt into each of 4 store-bought meringue nests. Drain 1 (15 oz) can apricots, thinly sliced, and arrange on top of the yogurt. Garnish each pavlova with a mint sprig. **Total cooking time 10 minutes.**

strawberry yogurt crunch

Serves **4**

Total cooking time **10 minutes**

¼ cup **strawberry preserves**

3 tablespoons packed **dark brown sugar**

2 cups **Greek yogurt**

8 **graham crackers**

1 small **chocolate-covered honeycomb toffee (sponge candy) bar**, broken into shards, or extra graham crackers, crushed, to decorate

Spoon the strawberry preserves into the bottom of 4 tall glasses. Stir the brown sugar into the Greek yogurt and divide half the mixture among the glasses.

Put the cookies into a plastic bag and smash with a rolling pin to form crumbs, then use the crumbs to cover the yogurt. Spoon the remaining yogurt over the crumbs and serve sprinkled with shards of chocolate-covered honeycomb toffee (sponge candy) or extra crushed cookies.

For marinated strawberry crunch, chop 8 oz hulled strawberries and mix with 1 teaspoon lemon juice, 1 tablespoon packed dark brown sugar, and the seeds scraped from ½ vanilla bean. Cover and set aside for 15 minutes. Meanwhile, put 8 graham crackers into a plastic bag and smash with a rolling pin. Divide the crumbs among 4 glass serving bowls. Top with 2 cups Greek yogurt, spoon the strawberries over the top, and serve immediately. **Total cooking time 25 minutes.**

blackberry brûlées

Serves **4**
Total cooking time **10 minutes**

1⅔ cups **blackberries**
2 tablespoons **apple juice**
2–3 teaspoons **granulated
  sugar**, to taste
½ cup **Greek yogurt**
2 tablespoons packed
  dark brown sugar

Put the blackberries, apple juice, and granulated sugar into a saucepan and simmer for 2–3 minutes. Spoon into 4 individual ramekins and let cool for 2–3 minutes.

Spoon the Greek yogurt over the berry mixture, then sprinkle with the brown sugar.

Cover and chill until required.

For blackberry mousse, put 2 cups blackberries, ¾ cup confectioners' sugar, and the juice of ½ lemon into a food processor or blender and process to a puree, then pass through a strainer into a large bowl. Stir in ⅔ cup heavy cream and ⅔ cup Greek yogurt and whip until thick. Divide among 4 dishes or glasses, then cover and chill for 10–12 minutes. Serve with dollops of plain yogurt and a few extra blackberries. **Total cooking time 20 minutes.**

mango & custard whips

Serves **4**

Total cooking time **20 minutes**

4 **firm, ripe, sweet mangoes**
1 cup canned **mango puree**
¼ cup **sugar**
⅔ cup **heavy cream**
½ teaspoon crushed
  cardamom seeds, plus extra
  to decorate
1 cup **fresh custard** or
  vanilla pudding

Pit and peel the mangoes, then cut the flesh into small bite-size cubes. Put three-quarters of the mango into a food processor or blender along with the mango puree and sugar and process until smooth.

Whip the cream with the cardamom seeds until it forms soft peaks and gently fold in the custard or vanilla pudding. Lightly fold one-quarter of the mango mixture into the custard mixture to create a marbled effect.

Divide half the reserved mango cubes among 4 individual serving glasses and top with half the cream mixture. Layer with two-thirds of the remaining mango mixture and top with the remaining cream mixture.

Decorate with the remaining mango mixture and cubes and a sprinkling of crushed cardamom seeds, then chill until ready to serve.

For mango & cardamom lassi, pit and peel 3 ripe mangoes and put the flesh into a food processor or blender with ¼ cup honey, 2 cups plain yogurt, and 1 teaspoon crushed cardamom seeds. Process until smooth, pour into 4 tall, ice-filled glasses, and serve. Total cooking time 10 minutes.

melting chocolate desserts

Serves **4**

Total cooking time **25 minutes**

4 oz **semisweet chocolate**

1 stick (4 oz) **butter**, plus extra
  for greasing

⅓ cup **superfine** or
  granulated sugar

2 **eggs**

2 tablespoons **unsweetened
  cocoa powder**

3 tablespoons **all-purpose
  flour**

confectioners' sugar,
  for dusting

Grease 4 large ramekins, about 3 inches in diameter. Melt the chocolate and butter in a small saucepan over low heat.

Meanwhile, beat the superfine or granulated sugar and eggs together until pale and creamy.

Pour the melted chocolate mixture into the egg mixture. Beat in the cocoa powder and flour, and continue beating until smooth.

Divide the mixture among the ramekins and cook in a preheated oven, at 350°F, for 10–12 minutes or until they are crisp on top and still melting inside.

Remove from the oven, set aside to cool for 1–2 minutes, then serve the desserts dusted with confectioners' sugar.

For vanilla ice cream with melting chocolate sauce, melt 6 oz semisweet chocolate, broken into pieces, with 1 tablespoon light corn syrup or maple syrup, 1 tablespoon butter, and ¼ cup water in a heatproof bowl over a saucepan of barely simmering water, making sure the bowl is not touching the surface of the water. Mix until smooth and glossy. Serve the sauce drizzled over vanilla ice cream. **Total cooking time 10 minutes.**

blackberry crisp

Serves **4**

Total cooking time **30 minutes**

5 cups **blackberries** (about
   1 ½ lb)
2 **oranges**, segmented
finely grated zest and juice
   of **1 orange**
1⅔ cups **all-purpose flour**
1¾ sticks (7 oz) **butter**, cubed
½ cup packed **light brown
   sugar**
cream, **ice cream**, or **custard**,
   to serve (optional)

Mix together the blackberries, orange segments, and
the orange zest and juice in a bowl.

Put the flour into a separate bowl, add the butter, and
rub in with your fingertips until the mixture resembles
bread crumbs, then stir in the sugar.

Transfer the blackberry mixture to a large pie dish and
sprinkle with the crumb mixture to cover.

Bake in a preheated oven, at 425°F, for 20–25 minutes,
until golden. Remove from the oven and serve warm
with cream, ice cream, or custard, if desired.

For blackberry, orange & custard desserts, divide
1 ¼ cups fresh custard or vanilla pudding among
4 dessert glasses. Process 1 ½ cups blackberries in
a food processor or blender with ¼ cup sugar until
smooth and spoon the blackberry puree over the
custard in the glasses. Peel and segment 2 large
oranges, then layer on top of the blackberry puree.
Top each glass with a small scoop of vanilla ice cream
and serve. **Total cooking time 10 minutes.**

mixed berry & meringue desserts

Serves **4**

Total cooking time **10 minutes**

1 (16 oz) package
  mixed berries, such as
  blackberries, raspberries,
  and blueberries, plus extra
  to decorate
1¾ cups **strawberry yogurt**
1¼ cups **crème fraîche**
  or **Greek yogurt**
¼ cup **confectioners' sugar**,
  sifted
4 **meringue nests**, coarsely
  crushed

Put half the berries into a food processor or blender and blend until smooth. Transfer to a bowl with the strawberry yogurt and stir to mix well.

Mix the remaining berries in a bowl with the crème fraîche or Greek yogurt and confectioners' sugar. Add to the berry and yogurt mixture and swirl through to create a marbled effect.

Fold in the crushed meringue and spoon into 4 chilled dessert glasses.

Serve immediately, decorated with berries.

For summer berry trifles, gently cook 1½ cups each raspberries, blueberries, and blackberries, ¼ cup sugar, and 2 tablespoons water in a small saucepan for 2–3 minutes, until the fruit is just soft. Let cool. Break 4 ladyfingers into small pieces and use to line 4 individual dessert bowls or glasses. Spoon the berry mixture over the ladyfingers, followed by 1 cup fresh custard vanilla or vanilla pudding. Top each with a spoonful of crème fraîche or Greek yogurt, cover, and chill until ready to serve. **Total cooking time 30 minutes.**

lemon–berry vanilla cream tart

Serves **4**

Total cooking time **10 minutes**

¾ cup **lemon curd**

1 (9 inch) **prepared tart shell**

8 oz **strawberries**, hulled and
  sliced (about 1⅔ cups)

1 **vanilla bean**, split
  lengthwise

1 cup **heavy cream**

1 tablespoon **confectioners'
  sugar**

Spread the lemon curd over the bottom of the tart shell,
then sprinkle with the sliced strawberries.

Scrape the seeds from the vanilla bean into the cream
with the confectioners' sugar and whip until it forms
soft peaks. Spoon over the strawberries and serve
immediately.

For lemon & vanilla mousse, put 1 cup heavy cream,
the seeds scraped from 1 vanilla bean, the grated zest
of 1 lemon, and ¼ cup sugar into a large bowl, then
whip until it forms soft peaks. Whisk 2 egg whites in
a separate, grease-free bowl until stiff and fold gently
into the cream with 3 tablespoons lemon curd. Spoon
another ⅔ cup lemon curd into 4 tall serving glasses,
then top with the mousse. Cover and chill in the
refrigerator for 15–20 minutes or until ready to serve.
Total cooking time 30 minutes.

cherry tiramisu

Serves **4**

Total cooking time **25 minutes**

⅓ cup **confectioners' sugar**, sifted

½ cup cold **strong black coffee**

12 **ladyfingers**

1 cup **mascarpone** or **ricotta cheese**

⅔ cup **heavy cream**

2 tablespoons **crème de cassis** or **syrup from canned cherries**

1 (15 oz) **can black cherries in light syrup**, drained

Stir 2 tablespoons of the confectioners' sugar into the coffee. Arrange the ladyfingers in the bottom of 4 individual glass dishes, then pour the black coffee over them and set aside to soak for about 5 minutes.

Meanwhile, beat the remaining confectioners' sugar into the mascarpone or ricotta cheese and heavy cream with the crème de cassis or cherry syrup.

Spoon the cheese mixture over the ladyfingers, cover, and chill in the refrigerator for 10–15 minutes. Spoon the drained cherries on top to serve.

For quick cherry tiramisu, divide 1 (15 oz) can cherry pie filling among 4 individual glass serving dishes. Beat ⅔ cup heavy cream with 1 ¼ cups Greek yogurt and 1 tablespoon honey until thickened, then crumble 6 ladyfingers into the mixture. Spoon onto the cherries and serve dusted with unsweetened cocoa powder. **Total cooking time 10 minutes.**

coconut rice with mango & lime

Serves **4**
Total cooking time **30 minutes**

⅔ cup **risotto rice**
⅓ cup **sugar**
1¼ cups **milk**
1¾ cups **coconut milk**
½ **mango**, pitted, peeled,
   and cut into small chunks
finely grated zest and juice
   of 1 **lime**
freshly grated **nutmeg**,
   to decorate

Put the rice into a heavy saucepan with the sugar, milk, and coconut milk. Bring to a boil, then reduce the heat and simmer for 20 minutes, until the rice has swelled and thickened.

Meanwhile, put the mango into a bowl and mix with the lime zest and juice.

Spoon the cooked rice into serving bowls and place spoonfuls of the mango and lime mixture into the center of each. Decorate with a little freshly grated nutmeg.

For coconut rice with caramelized banana, put ⅔ cup risotto rice into a heavy saucepan with ⅓ cup sugar, 1¼ cups milk, and 1¾ cups coconut milk. Bring to a boil, then reduce the heat and simmer for 20 minutes, until the rice has swelled and thickened. Meanwhile, cut 4 firm bananas in half lengthwise and sprinkle with ¼ cup packed light brown sugar and 1 teaspoon ground cinnamon. Heat a nonstick skillet over high heat and cook the bananas for 2 minutes on each side or until the sugar has caramelized. Spoon the cooked rice onto serving plates and top with the banana slices. **Total cooking time 25 minutes.**

scone & cream trifles

Serves **4**
Total cooking time **10 minutes**

1 cup hulled and quartered
   strawberries, plus 2 extra,
   halved, to decorate
¼ cup **strawberry preserves**
¼ cup **crème fraîche**,
   mascarpone, or **Greek**
   yogurt
2 **prepared scones**, halved

Put the strawberries into a bowl and mix with the strawberry preserves. Divide half the strawberries between the bottom of 4 serving glasses and top each with a spoonful of the cream and then a scone half.

Spoon the remaining strawberries over the top, then decorate each trifle with a strawberry half.

For scone & berry boozy trifle, put 8 oz strawberries, hulled (about 1 ½ cups), 1 cup raspberries, and ¼ cup strawberry or raspberry preserves into a bowl. Mix well, then transfer to a trifle bowl. Coarsely chop 4 prepared plain scones and sprinkle them over the fruit, then drizzle with ⅓ cup dry sherry. Spoon 2½ cups chilled prepared custard or vanilla pudding over the fruit, followed by 1¾ cup crème fraîche or whipped cream. Decorate with halved strawberries, if desired.
Total cooking time 15 minutes.

caramel pear upside-down tart

Serves **4–6**

Total cooking time **30 minutes**

butter, for greasing

2 (15 oz) cans **pears in fruit juice**, drained

⅓ cup **dulce de leche (caramel sauce)**

1 sheet **rolled dough piecrust**, defrosted if frozen

all-purpose flour, for dusting

ice cream or **cream**, to serve

Line the bottom of a 9 inch loose-bottom cake pan with parchment paper and grease.

Put the pears and dulce de leche (caramel sauce) into a saucepan and heat over gentle heat for 1–2 minutes, stirring occasionally, until the pears are well coated in the sauce. Arrange the pears in the bottom of the prepared pan in a single layer.

Roll out the dough on a lightly floured work surface to a circle slightly larger than the pan and place over the pears, folding any surplus down the side of the pan.

Put into a preheated oven, at 425°F, for 20 minutes, until the pastry is golden and cooked. Run a knife around the edge of the tart and turn out onto a serving plate. Serve cut into wedges with ice cream or cream.

For pan-fried caramelized pears, melt 2 tablespoons butter in a large, heavy skillet. Take 2 (15 oz) cans pears in fruit juice, drain and quarter the pears, and then place in a bowl. Coat the pears in ⅓ cup dulce de leche (caramel sauce) and cook in a skillet until the sauce is bubbling and the pears are softened. Serve with scoops of ice cream, drizzled with more sauce. **Total cooking time 10 minutes.**

berry, honey & yogurt desserts

Serves **4**
Total cooking time **10 minutes**

1 (16 oz) package **frozen
    mixed berries**, defrosted
juice of **1 orange**
⅓ cup **honey**
1¾ cups **vanilla yogurt**
½ cup **granola**

Process half the berries with the orange juice and honey in a food processor or blender until fairly smooth.

Transfer to a bowl and stir in the remaining berries.

Divide one-third of the berry mixture among 4 dessert glasses or small bowls. Top with half the yogurt.

Layer with half the remaining berry mixture and top with the remaining yogurt.

Top with the remaining berry mixture and sprinkle with the granola just before serving.

For berry & yogurt phyllo tarts, cut 2 large sheets of phyllo pastry in half and cut each half into 4 squares. Brush each square with melted butter. Stack 4 squares on top of each other and repeat with the remaining squares to create 4 stacks. Use to line four deep 4 inch tart pans. Bake the phyllo shells for 8–10 minutes in a preheated oven, at 350°F, until crispy and golden. Let cool and remove from the pans. To serve, place 2 tablespoons vanilla yogurt into each tart shell and divide 1½ cups mixed berries among them. Dust with confectioners' sugar and serve immediately. **Total cooking time 30 minutes.**

raspberry ripple pain perdu

Serves **4**

Total cooking time **20 minutes**

2⅔ cups **frozen raspberries**

1 teaspoon **lemon juice**

2 tablespoons **confectioners' sugar**, plus extra for dusting

2 **eggs**, lightly beaten

⅔ cup **superfine sugar**

1 teaspoon **vanilla extract** (optional)

1 cup **milk**

4 thick slices of day-old **country-style bread** or **brioche**

6 tablespoons **butter**

crème fraîche or **whipped cream**, to serve (optional)

Put the raspberries into a saucepan with the lemon juice and confectioners' sugar, and warm gently until just beginning to collapse. Process in a food processor or blender until smooth, then pass through a strainer to remove the seeds.

Whisk together the eggs, superfine sugar, and the vanilla extract, if using, in a bowl. Add the milk slowly, whisking until smooth and incorporated.

Dip the slices of bread in the egg mixture so that both sides are well coated. Melt the butter in a large, nonstick skillet and cook the egg-coated bread slices gently for about 2 minutes on each side, until crisp and golden.

Remove the bread from the pan and arrange on serving plates. Drizzle with the warm raspberry coulis to create a ripple effect, then dust with confectioners' sugar and serve immediately with crème fraîche or whipped cream, if desired.

For pain perdu with raspberry ripple ice cream, follow the recipe above to coat 4 thick slices of day-old country-style bread or brioche in the egg mixture and cook the bread slices until golden. Remove from the pan and sprinkle both sides of the bread with demerara or other raw sugar. Arrange on serving plates and top each slice with a scoop of raspberry ripple ice cream and a dusting of confectioners' sugar. **Total cooking time 10 minutes.**

almost instant peach trifle

Serves **4**

Total cooking time **10 minutes**

6 oz **store-bought raspberry jellyroll** or **pound cake**, sliced

1 (15 oz) can **sliced peaches in juice**, drained, juice reserved

¾ cup **mascarpone cheese**

1 cup **prepared custard** or **vanilla pudding**

2 tablespoons **confectioners' sugar**

⅔ cup **heavy cream**, whipped

3 tablespoons grated **milk** or **semisweet chocolate**, to decorate

Use the jellyroll or pound cake slices to line the bottom of an attractive glass serving dish. Drizzle with ½ cup of the reserved juice, then sprinkle with the sliced peaches.

Beat the mascarpone with the custard or vanilla pudding and confectioners' sugar in a bowl, then spoon it over the fruit.

Spoon the whipped cream over the top and decorate with the grated chocolate.

For baked peaches with mascarpone, cut 6 ripe but firm peaches or nectarines in half and remove the pits. Place the fruit, cut side up, in a snug-fitting ovenproof dish. Mix ½ cup orange juice with 2 tablespoons honey and pour the juice over the fruit. Sprinkle with 2 tablespoons confectioners' sugar and cook in a preheated oven, at 350°F, for 15–18 minutes, until tender. Meanwhile, beat 2 tablespoons confectioners' sugar into 1 cup mascarpone cheese, then cover and chill until required. Remove the fruit from the oven and arrange in serving dishes. Sprinkle with 1 cup raspberries, if desired, and serve with the sweetened mascarpone. **Total cooking time 30 minutes.**

almond affogato

4 scoops of **nougat** or **vanilla
ice cream**

4 drops of **almond extract**

4 shots of **hot strong coffee**

1 tablespoon **slivered
almonds**, toasted

almond cookies, to serve
(optional)

Put a scoop of ice cream into each of 4 heatproof
serving glasses.

Stir the almond extract into the hot coffee, then pour
1 shot over each scoop of ice cream.

Sprinkle with the toasted almonds and serve with
almond cookies, if desired.

For affogato-style tiramisu, stir 4 drops of almond
extract into ½ cup cold strong coffee. Arrange
16 ladyfingers in a dish, then pour the coffee over
them and set aside for 5 minutes to soak. Break up
the ladyfingers and divide half of them among 4 tall
freezer-proof glasses. Spoon a small scoop of nougat
or vanilla ice cream into each of the glasses, and
top with the remaining ladyfingers. Top with another
small scoop of ice cream, then put into the freezer for
10–15 minutes, until firm. Sprinkle with a dusting of
unsweetened cocoa powder and 1 tablespoon toasted
slivered almonds and serve with almond cookies, if
desired. **Total cooking time 30 minutes.**

index

acknowledgments

Commissioning editor: Eleanor Maxfield
Editor: Polly Poulter
Designer: Tracy Killick
Production controller: Allison Gonsalves
Indexer: Isobel McLean
Americanizer: Theresa Bebbington

Photography: Octopus Publishing Group Stephen Conroy 55, 69, 97, 127, 201, 203, 221, 223, 225; Will Heap 1, 2–3, 4–5, 6 left, 7, 8 left, 13, 17, 21, 25, 27, 31, 33, 37, 43, 49, 61, 79, 85, 87, 101, 111, 113, 117, 119, 131, 153, 161, 169, 171, 183, 189, 192–193, 195, 197, 209, 213, 215, 227; Lis Parsons 6 right, 10–11, 41, 45, 47, 52, 59, 63, 65, 71, 73, 75, 89, 91, 93, 95, 105, 115, 129, 139, 157, 163, 165, 191, 207; William Reavell 8 right, 9, 51, 67, 77, 81, 83, 99, 109, 159, 167, 199, 205, 211, 217, 219, 229, 231, 233; Craig Robertson 187; William Shaw 15, 19, 23, 29, 35, 39, 57, 107, 121, 123, 125, 133, 135, 137, 141, 143, 145, 147, 149, 155, 173, 175, 177, 179, 181, 185; Ian Wallace 102–103, 150–151.